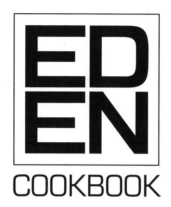

COOKBOOK

Eleanor Walsh and Michael Durkin

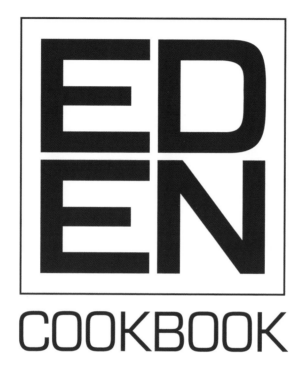

COOKBOOK

GILL & MACMILLAN

Gill & Macmillan Ltd
Hume Avenue
Park West
Dublin 12
with associated companies throughout the world
www.gillmacmillan.ie

978 07171 9229 3

Photographs by Hugh McElveen
Photograph on page xiv by Pierce Tynan
Index compiled by Cover to Cover

Book design and typesetting by Anú Design, Tara
Printed by GraphyCems, Spain

The paper used in this book is made from the wood pulp of managed forests.
For every tree felled, at least one tree is planted,
thereby renewing natural resources.

A CIP catalogue record is available for this book from the British Library.

1 3 5 4 2

Contents

Bakery

Soup

Fish

Meat

So You Don't Eat Meat

Ice Cream and Puddings

Sheridan's Cheese

Cocktails

Conversion Charts

Weight			Volume	
10 g	½ oz		5 ml	1 teaspoon
20 g	¾ oz		10 ml	1 dessertspoon
25 g	1 oz		15 ml	1 tablespoon
50 g	2 oz		30 ml	1 fl oz
60 g	2½ oz		50 ml	2 fl oz
75 g	3 oz		75 ml	3 fl oz
100 g	3½ oz		100 ml	3½ fl oz
110 g	4 oz		125 ml	4 fl oz
150 g	5 oz		150 ml	5 fl oz (¼ pint)
175 g	6 oz		200 ml	7 fl oz (⅓ pint)
200 g	7 oz		250 ml	9 fl oz
225 g	8 oz		300 ml	10 fl oz
250 g	9 oz		350 ml	12 fl oz
275 g	10 oz		400 ml	14 fl oz
350 g	12 oz		425 ml	15 fl oz (¾ pint)
400 g	14 oz		450 ml	16 fl oz
450 g	1 lb		500 ml	18 fl oz
500 g	18 oz		600 ml	1 pint
600 g	1¼ lb		700 ml	1¼ pints
700 g	1½ lb		850 ml	1½ pints
900 g	2 lb		1 litre	1¾ pints
1 kg	2¼ lb		1.2 litres	2 pints
1.1 kg	2½ lb		1.5 litres	2½ pints
1.3 kg	3 lb		1.8 litres	3 pints
1.5 kg	3 lb 5 oz		2 litres	3½ pints
1.6 kg	3½ lb			
1.8 kg	4 lb			
2 kg	4½ lb			
2.2 kg	5 lb			

Introduction

Ingredients come first with me. Using the best-quality ingredients will add an extra dimension to your food. Let your cooking be about the food and not what you do with it. Good food needs very little interference.

I love food, but the most important ingredients are friends, family and fun to create a truly memorable meal. Food is life and has to be shared to be truly appreciated.

I love cooking and so many dishes are inspired by raw ingredients; risotto will be inspired by fresh truffles, Welsh rarebit by a visit to Sheridan's cheese-mongers and all fish dishes by a walk down Dingle pier. The produce we use in Eden is carefully sourced. It is a joy to work with suppliers who care about and believe in their produce.

I was incredibly lucky to be born in Dingle, surrounded by good food that was easily accessible. No air miles there. My mum, Oige, understood and nurtured my love of cooking and taught me all she knew. Her mother, Ellie Curran (nee Rayel), ran an amazing butcher shop next door, ably assisted by Michael Lovett. I worked there every summer and learned how to butcher meat, make blood pudding, smoke bacon, cure sheepskins and countless other things. I definitely got my 'waste not' philosophy from her. She also had her own kitchen garden. Digging spuds half an hour before they were cooked with a sprig of mint is an incredible memory.

A chef's success invariably depends on the skill and dedication of others. Eden was conceived in the summer of 1996 and came to life in March 1997. Jay Bourke and Eoin Foyle approached me to set up a restaurant with them. At the time I was cooking in Cookes, where Johnny was showing Dublin just how it could be done.

In Eden we wanted to use the best of Irish produce, design and people, and ten years later I think we've achieved this.

So many people have helped Eden to reach its tenth birthday and I am truly

grateful to everyone. It would be impossible to mention everybody, but you all know who you are and the role you played. My thanks to a dedicated, loyal and hard-working kitchen team led by Mick, ably assisted by Greg, Brian, Cathy, Tara and their teams. Huge credit to Mick Durkin, who took over from me in the kitchen in 2001 as head chef and enabled me to step back and work on Café Bar Deli. It was a difficult move for me, but Mick has always been very patient with my constant interference. The Market Bar and Mackerel would not have happened without him stepping into and more than filling my shoes in Eden. He also helped pull this book together and made sure we met all deadlines.

Our new baby, Eden 2, in Bellinter House, Co. Meath is keeping me occupied now. The Eden country experience will enable us to grow our own vegetables and herbs. The garden should come on line this year and will add another dimension to Eden.

The journey has been fun thus far, and cooking for people is a gift from the cook to the table. Good food only happens when you truly put yourself into it. These recipes are meant to inspire, so don't be afraid of failure. We alter things all the time and this makes our work interesting. Please feel free to swap ingredients and use these recipes as a spring board for your own culinary journey.

If you are a novice, read the recipe in its entirety a few days before you plan to cook it. This will ensure you start on time and have all the necessary equipment and ingredients. Also, each oven is different and you must learn your oven's little whims. If you are using a fan oven, it will cook more quickly and you should reduce the temperature in the recipe by 20 degrees.

I have not included a separate chapter on appetisers, as I have covered all dishes in the fish, meat and vegetable chapters. I believe the way we eat has changed and we no longer eat a three-course meal as formally as we did. Most dishes can be served in smaller or larger portions depending on how hungry you and your guests are.

I want this cookbook to be worn and used, with recipe cut-outs and hand-scribbled notes in it. Please use it and pass it on.

Above all, enjoy the food experience. It is meant to be fun and give you a sense of achievement.

A special mention in memory of Leahy, a man who truly loved life, food and Eden; thanks for all your support in the early days.

Eleanor Walsh
March 2007
www.edenrestaurant.ie

Larder

Aioli, hollandaise and béarnaise are the three main raw egg sauces we use in Eden, along with sauce Anglaise, a sweet sauce in the pastry section. People tend to be afraid of these sauces, as they are prone to curdling and splitting – horrible, scary words when you want to cook to impress. Two top tips: take your time and have the eggs at room temperature. Also, as you are using raw eggs, make sure they are fresh.

Hollandaise Sauce

Serves 6

3 tablespoons white wine vinegar
3 egg yolks
120 g butter at room temperature
Salt and ground white pepper

Place the vinegar in a saucepan and reduce amount by half by boiling. Bring a saucepan of water to boil and cover with a tea towel (the tea towel will stop the bowl from slipping). Place the egg yolks in a bowl. Add the vinegar and stand the bowl over boiling water. Whisk until it holds a figure 8. What you are doing is cooking the eggs without scrambling them.

Add the softened butter, cube by cube, to the egg mix, making sure each cube is whisked in before you add the next one. Again, do not rush this stage. Alternatively, you can melt the butter and add it very slowly, as you do the oil when making mayonnaise. Check seasoning. Covered with cling film and kept warm, this sauce will hold for 90 minutes, but ideally should be used as soon as possible.

Aioli

2 egg yolks
2 tablespoons white wine vinegar
3 cloves of garlic, finely chopped
½ teaspoon salt
125 ml olive oil
125 ml sunflower oil

In a food processor or blender, whisk the egg yolks, vinegar, garlic and salt. Mix the oils together, and add drop by drop to the egg mix until the mixture has thickened. Do not rush this process. Check seasoning and store in the fridge. Use within 3 days. Freshly chopped herbs and lime juice can be added to give extra flavour; dill or chives are good.

Béarnaise Sauce

Serves 6

To be served with steak and chips (or on a slice of white bread as a sneaky snack in the kitchen).

50 ml tarragon vinegar
2 teaspoons chopped shallot
1 tablespoon chopped tarragon
3 egg yolks
150 g butter
1 teaspoon chopped chervil (optional)
Pinch of freshly ground white pepper

In a saucepan over a moderate heat, reduce the vinegar, shallot and tarragon to a tablespoon. Strain into the egg yolks and follow the method on p. 5 for hollandaise. Add the chopped herbs before serving.

Baba Ghanoush

2 aubergines
2 tablespoons olive oil, for baking aubergine
Juice of 1 lemon
1 clove of crushed garlic
1 tablespoon chopped flat-leaf parsley
1 tablespoon chopped coriander
Sprinkle of chilli powder
2 teaspoons tahini paste
Salt and freshly ground white pepper

Preheat the oven to 200°C/400°F/gas 6.

Rub the skin of the aubergines with olive oil. Place on a baking tray and bake until skin is blistered. This will take about 30 minutes; turn them after 15 minutes. Allow aubergine to cool in a sieve or colander over a bowl. This will allow any bitter juices to drain off. Peel and drain for a further 5 minutes. Place all ingredients in a blender and blend until smooth. Check seasoning. This will last for 3 days covered with a thin layer of olive oil. Store in the fridge.

Black Bean Salsa

Serves 6

175 g black turtle beans, soaked overnight in cold water
1 red onion, peeled and finely diced
1 red chilli, deseeded and finely diced
1 red pepper, finely diced
1 yellow pepper, finely diced
3 drops Tabasco, or to taste
1 tablespoon olive oil
Juice and zest of 2 limes
3 tablespoons fresh coriander, chopped
Salt and freshly ground black pepper

Rinse beans and place in a saucepan. Cover with cold water and bring to the boil, reduce the heat and simmer until the beans are tender, approximately 25 minutes. Drain and cool with cold water. Mix all the ingredients in a bowl. Add the beans and mix well. Serve. We serve this salsa on its own as a salad or use it as a base for fish or chicken.

Chickpea Relish

150 g chickpeas, soaked in cold water overnight
100 ml extra virgin olive oil
1 red onion, finely diced
2 cloves of garlic, crushed
1 tablespoon chopped ginger
1 red chilli, finely diced
½ teaspoon cumin seeds
½ teaspoon coriander seeds
100 g chopped tinned tomatoes
2 red peppers, finely diced
1 tablespoon brown sugar
1 tablespoon balsamic vinegar
1 tablespoon tomato purée
1 tablespoon chopped mint, to garnish
1 tablespoon chopped coriander, to garnish

Cover the chickpeas with cold water in a saucepan. Bring to the boil and simmer until tender. Drain and cool with cold water. In a large saucepan, heat the olive oil and fry the onion, garlic, ginger, chilli and spices until soft. Add the remaining ingredients, season and bring to the boil. Reduce the heat, add the chickpeas and cover. Cook over a gentle heat for 20 minutes. Stir to prevent the relish from sticking. Add a little water if the mixture is getting too thick. Cool to room temperature and add chopped mint and coriander before serving.

Chilli Jam

275 g granulated sugar
100 ml white wine vinegar
½ cinnamon stick
½ vanilla pod
1 teaspoon sunflower oil
1 onion, peeled and finely diced
250 g red chilli, sliced (remove seeds for less heat)
1 red pepper, deseeded and finely diced
1 tablespoon tomato purée
2 teaspoons chopped ginger
1 teaspoon chopped garlic

Place the sugar, white wine vinegar, cinnamon stick and vanilla pod in a saucepan. Dissolve the sugar, then boil to make a syrup golden in colour. In another saucepan, heat the oil and cook the remaining ingredients until soft. Add the syrup to the tomato purée. This can be blended for a smoother paste or left as is for chunky relish. Stored in an airtight jar in the fridge, this will last for 1 month.

Pickled Chillies

250 g red chillies
1 jar of honey
250 ml rice wine vinegar

100 g caster sugar
Juice of 2 limes
6 juniper berries

Remove the green stalk from the chillies and slice at an angle. (Again, remove the seeds for less heat if you wish.) Place all the other ingredients in a saucepan and bring to the boil, then simmer for 5 minutes. Remove from heat. Add the chillies to the hot liquid. Cool and refrigerate. This will keep for 2 weeks.

Compound Butters

I make these in 1-lb batches and keep them in the freezer. They can be served on chicken, fish and steak, or simply with bread. They will keep for 3 months in the freezer and you can just slice off as much as you need. With these in the freezer, you will never be short of a quick sauce.

Red Wine Shallot Butter

3 shallots, finely chopped
1 cup of red wine
450 g butter at room temperature
2 tablespoons chopped thyme or rosemary

Place the shallots and red wine in a saucepan. Reduce over a medium heat until all the wine has evaporated. At this stage the shallots should be shiny and dark red in colour. Cool. Place the butter, shallots and herbs in a food processor and blend. Roll the butter into a sausage shape in greaseproof paper. Place in freezer.

Hazelnut, Lemon and Herb Butter

450 g butter at room temperature
100 g toasted hazelnuts
2 tablespoons chopped parsley
Zest and juice of 1 lemon

Place all the ingredients in a food processor and blend. Roll the butter into a sausage shape in greaseproof paper. Store in the freezer.

Lime, Chilli and Coriander Butter

450 g butter at room temperature
Juice and zest of 3 limes
3 tablespoons chopped coriander
2 red chillies, deseeded and diced, or 2 tablespoons of harissa
(a sweet chilli paste available in Asian markets)

Place all the ingredients in a food processor and blend. Roll the butter into a sausage shape in greaseproof paper. Store in the freezer.

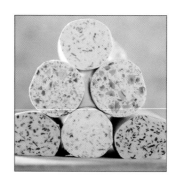

House Salad Dressing

1 teaspoon wholegrain mustard
1 teaspoon honey
120 ml sunflower oil
60 ml olive oil
60 ml tarragon vinegar
Salt and freshly ground black pepper
¼ clove of garlic, diced

Place all the ingredients in a clean glass jar with a tight-fitting lid and shake for 5 minutes. This dressing will hold for 1 week in your fridge. Shake well before using.

Sesame and Ginger Dressing

2 teaspoons toasted sesame seeds
1 teaspoon chopped pickled ginger (available in Asian supermarkets)
1 clove of garlic, finely chopped
90 ml arachide oil
90 ml sesame seed oil
50 ml rice wine vinegar
50 ml soy sauce (we use Kikkoman)
Freshly ground black pepper

Place all the ingredients in a clean glass jar with a tight-fitting lid and shake for 5 minutes. This dressing will hold for 1 week in your fridge. Shake before using.

Balsamic Dressing

6 tablespoons cold-pressed olive oil
2 tablespoons 12-year-old balsamic vinegar
Salt and freshly ground black pepper

Place all the ingredients in a clean glass jar with a tight-fitting lid and shake for 5 minutes.

Balsamic Reduction

Place 500 ml balsamic vinegar in a saucepan over a moderate heat. Reduce by half. This will give you a thick syrup which can be used to garnish dishes and decorate plates. Store in a plastic squeezy bottle in the fridge.

Hummus

An essential stock item, this is a great dip for bread, raw vegetables or a topping for fish or chicken. Couldn't live without it.

240 g chickpeas
4 cloves of garlic, finely chopped
Juice of 1 lemon
Salt and pepper

½ teaspoon ground cumin
2 tablespoons tahini paste
100 ml olive oil
100 ml sunflower oil

Rinse and soak chickpeas in cold water for 24 hours. Place in a saucepan, cover with cold water, bring to the boil and simmer until tender, about 40 minutes. Remove from heat and drain. Place the chickpeas, garlic, lemon juice, salt and pepper, cumin and tahini paste in a blender. Slowly add oil until blended. If it's too thick, add a little water. Check seasoning and store in an airtight container in the fridge, where it will keep for 5 days. You can also add some harissa (sweet chilli paste) to mix in at the end, which will give you a chilli hummus.

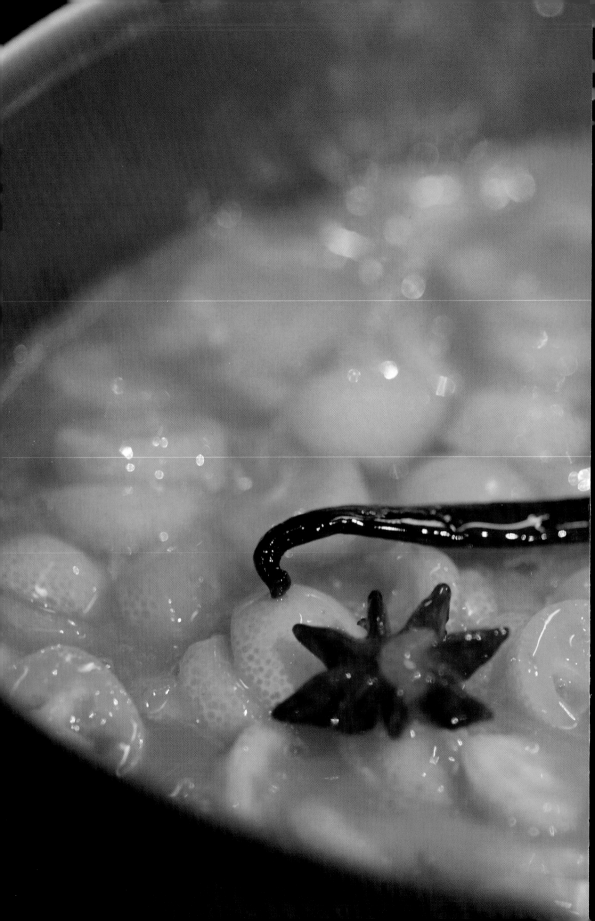

Kumquat Relish

This is fantastic with duck or cheese.

½ litre orange juice
1 vanilla pod
4 whole star anise
1 tablespoon chopped fresh ginger
1 red chilli, deseeded and sliced
2 tablespoons sugar
1 kilo kumquats, sliced and pips removed

Put the orange juice, vanilla pod, star anise, ginger, chilli and sugar in a saucepan. Dissolve the sugar over a low heat and then bring to the boil. Simmer for 10 minutes. Add the kumquats and simmer for a further 10 minutes, until tender but still holding their shape. If the relish needs to be thicker, dissolve 1 teaspoon of arrowroot in 3 teaspoons of cold water and add to the hot relish. Cool and store in an airtight container in the fridge, where it will keep for 3 weeks.

Onion Marmalade

Another Eden basic, always on hand. This is excellent with cheese, any roast meat, pâtés and terrines. Also makes an excellent sauce for meat dishes if you add jus.

1 kg white or red onions
3 tablespoons sunflower oil
200 g brown sugar
2 teaspoons salt
2 teaspoons freshly ground white pepper
9 tablespoons white wine vinegar (use balsamic vinegar if you want a darker colour)

Peel the onions and cut in half, through the root. Slice thinly and evenly. Heat the oil in a saucepan. Add the onion, sugar, salt and pepper and stir well. Cover with a lid and cook for 30 minutes over a gentle heat. Stir from time to time to prevent the onions from sticking. Remove lid and add the vinegar and cook for a further 30 minutes over a low heat. Stir regularly. Cool and place in a jar with a tightly fitted lid. This will keep for 2 weeks in the fridge.

Oven-Dried Tomatoes

These are fantastic in salads, quiche, served with roast chicken, a steak sandwich or on their own with white bread. Make at least twice the quantity at the time and store in an airtight container covered with olive oil. They will last for a week.

20 g Maldon sea salt
8 plum tomatoes, halved
2 tablespoons olive oil
2 shallots, peeled and finely chopped
2 cloves of garlic, peeled and sliced
1 sprig of rosemary, roughly chopped
1 sprig of thyme, roughly chopped
10 g caster sugar

Preheat the oven to 100°C/200°F/gas mark ½.

Sprinkle salt on a baking tray. Place the tomatoes on the salt, skin side down. Mix all the other ingredients together and sprinkle over the tomatoes. Place in the oven for 6 hours.

Peperonata

Excellent with chicken, fish and cold meats.

100 ml olive oil
1 onion, halved and sliced
6 cloves of garlic, peeled and sliced
3 red peppers, deseeded and cut into strips
3 yellow peppers, deseeded and cut into strips
1 red chilli, deseeded and finely sliced
3 tomatoes, each cut into 6 wedges
3 tablespoons stoned kalamata olives
Salt and freshly ground white pepper
1 tablespoon roughly chopped basil

Heat a thick-based pan and add the olive oil. Add the onion and garlic and cook over a low heat until soft. Add the peppers and chilli, cover and cook gently for 10 minutes, until soft. Add the tomatoes and olives and season. Turn off the heat and allow to sit for 15 minutes. Serve warm with chopped basil.

Pickled Lemons

Adds great flavour to tagines, couscous and chicken dishes.

4 lemons, unwaxed if possible
100 g caster sugar
300 ml water
200 ml white wine vinegar

Wash lemons and slice in circles as thin as a match stick. Remove pips. Put the sugar, water and vinegar in a saucepan. Dissolve the sugar over a low heat and then bring to the boil. Boil for 5 minutes. Remove from the heat, add the sliced lemon and cool. Store in an airtight container in the fridge. This will last for 1 month if properly stored.

Pickled Cucumber

Great for picnics, with gravadlax, poached salmon or a ploughman's lunch.

100 g caster sugar
170 ml rice wine vinegar
10 juniper berries
½ teaspoon coriander seeds

2 whole star anise
Zest and juice of 1 lemon
3 cucumbers
2 tablespoons chopped dill

To make the syrup, place the sugar, vinegar, juniper berries, coriander seeds, star anise and lemon zest and juice in a saucepan over a gentle heat. Dissolve the sugar and bring to the boil, then simmer for 5 minutes. Remove from the heat and cool. If the skin of the cucumber is thick, remove with a vegetable peeler. I prefer to leave skin on for a contrast of colour and texture. Slice cucumbers thinly and add to the cold syrup, along with the dill. Store in the fridge in an airtight jar. This will keep for 1 week, but the colour will fade as time passes.

Curry Oil

Great drizzled on fish or brushed on pitta bread before grilling.

2 cloves of garlic, peeled and sliced
3 tablespoons curry powder
1 teaspoon ground turmeric
1 teaspoon coriander seeds
2 cardamom pods
2 lime leaves
300 ml olive oil

Heat a saucepan and add all the ingredients except the oil. Heat gently to bring out the flavours. Add the oil and simmer for 10 minutes. Remove from heat and cool. Pour into an airtight container and leave for 48 hours. Strain into a bottle and store.

Red Pepper Relish

A favourite with chicken, fish, roast vegetables or sandwiches. Always a good one to have in stock.

2 tablespoons sunflower oil
2 red onions, peeled and finely diced
3 cloves of garlic, crushed
1 tablespoon chopped fresh ginger
8 red peppers, deseeded and finely diced
Salt and freshly ground white pepper
1 x 400 g tin chopped plum tomatoes
300 g brown sugar
200 ml white wine vinegar
1 teaspoon mustard seeds
½ teaspoon coriander seeds

Heat the oil in a large saucepan. Add the onion, garlic, ginger and peppers. Cook for 5 minutes. Season with salt and pepper. Add the remaining ingredients and simmer gently for 90 minutes on a low heat. Stir from time to time to stop mixture from sticking. Make sure the liquid doesn't evaporate, or the relish will burn. If necessary, add a little cold water. Check seasoning. Cool and store in an airtight container in the fridge. This will keep for 10 days.

Salsa Verde

This is best made by hand by chopping the herbs very finely. An all-rounder, great with chicken, fish and steak.

2 handfuls flat-leaf parsley
1 handful basil leaves
1 handful mint leaves
2 cloves of garlic, peeled and crushed
1 tablespoon capers, finely chopped
1 tablespoon gherkins, finely chopped
5 anchovy fillets, finely chopped
1 tablespoon Dijon mustard
2 tablespoons red wine vinegar
120 ml extra virgin olive oil
Freshly ground white pepper

Chop the herbs finely. Mix the herbs, garlic, capers, gherkins and anchovies in a bowl. Add the mustard and vinegar and mix well. Slowly stir in the oil. Season with pepper; you may not need salt. Some traditional Italian recipes add white bread to this, which softens the texture and flavour. Covered in the fridge, this will last for 5 days, but the colour will darken.

Beef/Veal Stock

Makes 5 litres of stock

This is the basis of most stews and sauces in Eden. It's acceptable to use a good-quality stock cube such as Kallo or Marigold if you're in a hurry. I know people who use a tin of consommé in the home kitchen; just taste it first, as it can be salty and affect the amount of salt you will add to a stew. However, a good beef or veal stock will add a huge dimension to stews and meat sauces. We always have a beef stock on the stove in Eden and the following is a simpler recipe for this stock. It will freeze and is worth the effort. Do not attempt unless you have a large saucepan, possibly the one you use for the Christmas ham.

3 kg shin bone of beef (ask your butcher to save these for you)
2 tablespoons sunflower oil
3 large Spanish onions, skin on and halved
2 cloves of garlic
3 stalks of celery
4 carrots, broken in three
1 leek, chopped
1 tablespoon tomato purée
1 sprig rosemary
1 sprig thyme
10 whole black peppercorns
1 tablespoon balsamic vinegar
6½ litres water

Preheat the oven to 200°C/400°F/gas 6.

Place bones in a roasting tray and brown, 30 to 40 minutes. Meanwhile, heat the sunflower oil in a saucepan and brown the onions until dark brown but not burned. Add the garlic, celery, carrots and leek. Cook until brown. Add the tomato purée, herbs, peppercorns and balsamic vinegar. Finally, add the bones and water, bring to the boil and skim off any froth and discard. Reduce the heat and simmer for 8 hours, skimming when necessary. As you may have gathered, this is a slow process, but when the time is up, get help to lift the saucepan and strain the liquid. **Remember, you want to keep the liquid and discard the bones.** I have seen many stocks being thrown away by an unknowing junior wondering what we do next with the bones they have carefully kept.

This is now a rich beef stock which can be used in stews and rich beef soups. To make a jus, which we use in all our meat sauces, we return the stock to the saucepan with a bottle of red wine and reduce the liquid slowly to 1½ litres. A lot of effort, but a lot of flavour gained. This is worthwhile work. This will keep in the fridge for 1 week or freeze for 3 months. If freezing, divide into four portions, as it is unlikely you will use all the jus for one dish.

Tapenade

Fantastic with chicken, roast hake, goat's cheese, tomatoes or as a dip with bread; the list is endless.

3 cloves of garlic, crushed
250 g stoned black olives
2 tablespoons capers
1 dessertspoon mustard
4 anchovy fillets (optional, but they do add great flavour)
150 ml olive oil
1 teaspoon lemon juice
Freshly ground black pepper

Place the garlic, olives, capers, mustard and anchovies in a blender to make a paste. Put the blender on low speed and add the oil slowly. Add the lemon juice and pepper. It's unlikely you will need salt, as olives, capers and anchovies are quite salty foods already. Store in an airtight container, covered with a thin layer of olive oil. This will last for weeks.

Tomato Pesto

20 large sun-dried tomatoes
1 tablespoon Dijon mustard
4 tablespoons white wine vinegar
1 tablespoon crushed garlic

50 g toasted pine nuts
Salt and freshly ground black pepper
250 ml sunflower oil
250 ml olive oil

Place the first 5 ingredients in a blender. Mix to a paste. Slowly add the sunflower and olive oil on low speed. Season to taste. Stored in an airtight container in the fridge, this will keep for 10 days.

Tomato Sauce

An Eden staple. Can be used as a basic pasta sauce, a base for fish stew, a topping for roast aubergine, a pizza base (if reduced) and many other dishes. Great if made in summer when tomatoes are full of flavour.

2 tablespoons olive oil
1 large onion, finely diced
2 cloves of garlic, chopped
Salt and freshly ground white pepper
6 vine-ripe tomatoes, cut in quarters
4 tablespoons white wine
250 ml water or vegetable stock
1 x 400 g tin of Italian plum tomatoes
Pinch of sugar
Handful of fresh basil leaves, roughly torn

Heat the oil in a large heavy-bottomed saucepan and gently cook the onion and garlic. Add salt and pepper. Add the vine-ripe tomatoes and white wine and cook for 15 minutes. Add the stock/water, tinned tomatoes and sugar. Simmer gently for 25 minutes. Cool and add the basil. If you want a finer sauce, pass through a sieve. This sauce will keep for 3 days in the fridge and can also be frozen.

Tzatziki

1 cucumber
1 teaspoon salt
450 g Greek-style yoghurt
1 clove of garlic, finely chopped
1 handful mint leaves, chopped
Freshly ground pepper

Grate the cucumber into a sieve. Add 1 teaspoon of salt, mix and allow to stand for 5 minutes. Rinse well with cold water and gently squeeze dry. Combine all the ingredients in a bowl and season. Leave for 20 minutes before serving to allow the flavour to develop.

Horseradish Crème Fraîche

250 ml crème fraîche
½ clove of garlic, crushed
1 tablespoon horseradish sauce
Juice of half a lemon
Salt and freshly ground black pepper

Combine all the ingredients. Leave for 20 minutes before serving to allow the flavour to develop.

Bakery

Eden Brown Bread

Makes 2 loaves

225 g strong white flour
15 g salt
2 teaspoons bread soda
225 g wholemeal flour
30 g bran
30 g wheat germ
30 g pinhead oatmeal and another 20 g to sprinkle on top
30 g brown sugar
600 ml buttermilk
1 tablespoon sunflower oil

Preheat the oven to 190°C/375°F/gas 5. Butter and flour 2 x 2-lb loaf tins. In a large bowl, sieve the white flour, salt and bread soda. Add all the other dry ingredients. Make a well in the centre and add the buttermilk and oil. Use your hand to mix all the ingredients together. The dough will be quite wet. Avoid over-mixing, as this will make the bread chewy. Divide into the prepared tins and sprinkle with the 20 g pinhead oatmeal. Bake for 90 minutes. Test with a skewer to ensure centre isn't wet. Remove from tin and cool on a wire rack.

Guinness Bread

Makes 2 loaves

Excellent with oysters, chowder, gravadlax and smoked mackerel pâté.

250 g strong white flour
2 tablespoons bread soda
2 teaspoons salt
1 kg wholemeal flour
600 ml buttermilk

250 ml Guinness
250 g treacle
50 ml oil
30 g porridge flakes

Preheat the oven to 190°C/375°F/gas 5. Butter and flour 2 x 2-lb loaf tins.
In a large bowl, sieve the strong white flour, bread soda and salt. Add the
wholemeal flour. Make a well and add in all the liquid. Mix gently with a
wooden spoon and pour into the prepared tins. Flatten the mixture on top
and sprinkle with porridge flakes. Bake for 90 minutes. Remove from tin
and cool on a wire tray.

White Soda Bread

Makes 2 loaves

900 g plain flour
2 teaspoons salt
2 flat teaspoons bread soda
850 ml buttermilk

Preheat the oven to 200°C/400°F/gas 6. Sieve the dry ingredients into a bowl.
Make a well in the centre and add the buttermilk. Mix with your hand until
it all comes together. Turn the dough out onto a floured surface and knead
gently. Cut into two. Shape the dough into rounds about 4 cm thick. Dust
with flour and mark with a cross in the centre. Bake for 30 minutes, or until
hollow when tapped.

Eden Banana Bread

Makes 1 loaf

Delicious and makes fantastic bread and butter pudding if there are leftovers, which is unlikely!

225 g lightly mashed banana (weight with skin removed)
225 g caster sugar
2 eggs
225 g self-raising flour
1 level teaspoon baking powder

Preheat the oven to 190°C/375°F/gas 5. Butter and flour a 2-lb loaf tin. Line the bottom with silicone paper. Mix the bananas and sugar together. Add the eggs and mix gently. Sieve in the flour and baking powder. Mix well until all the flour is incorporated. It will look like a thick batter. Pour into the prepared tin and bake for 1 hour. Remove from the oven but allow to cool in the tin. When cold, remove from the tin.

Beer Bread

Makes 1 loaf

400 g self-raising flour   *2 tablespoons caster sugar*
10 g salt   *325 ml beer*

Preheat the oven to 190°C/375°F/gas 5. Grease a 2-lb loaf tin. Combine the flour, salt and sugar in a large bowl. Slowly add three-quarters of the beer, mixing with a wooden spoon until the mixture is a wet batter. Add more beer if necessary. Pour into tin. Bake for 40 minutes, until the top is a golden brown. Remove from the oven and cool in the tin for 10 minutes, then remove from tin and cool on a wire tray.

Spelt Bread

Makes 2 loaves

2 sachets fast-acting dried yeast
400 ml tepid water (37°C/98.6°F)
1 kg spelt flour
25 g sea salt

50 g honey
1 tablespoon mixed seeds (we use
sunflower, sesame and linseeds)
Olive oil

Preheat the oven to 190°C/375°F/gas 5. Oil 2 x 2-lb loaf tins. Put 40 ml warm water in a bowl, add the honey, crumble the yeast on top and leave to stand for a few minutes, until it bubbles on top. This shows the yeast is active and will rise your bread. Sieve the flour and salt into a large bowl. Make a hole in the middle of the flour. Add the honey and yeast mix, then the remaining tepid water. Mix into a dough. Cover with cling film and allow to double in size in a warm place. Place the dough on a floured work top and knock back to original size. Shape into 2 loaf tins, put in a warm place and allow to double in size again. Brush loaves lightly with olive oil and sprinkle loaves with mixed seeds. Bake for 40 minutes.

Corn Bread

This makes a great alternative to wheat bread and is gluten free.

300 g fine polenta
4 teaspoons baking powder
(gluten free)
½ teaspoon salt
100 g grated Parmesan

1 tablespoon chopped herbs
225 ml milk
3 eggs
5 tablespoons sunflower oil

Preheat the oven to 200°C/400°F/gas 6. Oil a square 18 cm cake tin. Place the polenta in a large bowl. Sieve in the baking powder. Add the salt and mix well with a wooden spoon. Add the grated cheese and herbs. Mix the milk, eggs and oil together in a jug. Pour into the polenta and mix together to form a wet dough. Pour the dough into the oiled tin and bake for 25 minutes, until golden brown and springy to the touch. Remove from the tin. Cool on a wire tray.

White Yeast Bread

Makes 1 loaf

30 ml + 170–180 ml water at 37°C/98.6°F
1 sachet fast-acting dried yeast
300 g strong flour
10 g salt
10 g caster sugar

Preheat the oven to 200°C/400°F/gas 6. Oil and flour a 2-lb loaf tin. Put 30 ml warm water in a bowl, crumble the yeast on top and leave to stand for a few minutes, until it bubbles on top. This shows the yeast is alive and will rise your bread. With an electric mixer, mix the flour, salt and sugar together in a bowl. Add the yeast to the flour mix and mix thoroughly. Add the remaining water gradually, with the machine on a low speed, for about 5 minutes. Increase speed for 10 minutes, until you have a smooth, elastic dough. (If you are making the bread by hand, once all the liquid is added, you will have to knead the dough for at least 10 minutes.) Place in a clean bowl and cover with a clean tea towel. Leave to double in size. Remove from the bowl onto a lightly floured surface and knock back and shape into a 2-lb loaf tin. Allow to prove again in the tin, until doubled in size, and bake for 40 minutes. Remove from tin and cool.

Herb Yeast Bread

Makes 1 loaf

For the basil and sage purée:
2 handfuls sage leaves
2 handfuls basil leaves
2 tablespoons olive oil

For the bread:
30 ml + 120 ml tepid water at 37°C/98.6°F
1 sachet fast-acting dried yeast
60 g basil and sage purée
300 g strong flour
10 g salt
10 g caster sugar

To make the basil and sage purée, blend the herbs and oil together until smooth. For the bread, preheat the oven to 200°C/400°F/gas 6. Follow the method of White Yeast Bread (p. 45). Add the herb purée when you are adding the tepid water. This bread may take slightly longer to prove, as the oil in the herb paste will make the dough heavier, which means the yeast has a harder job.

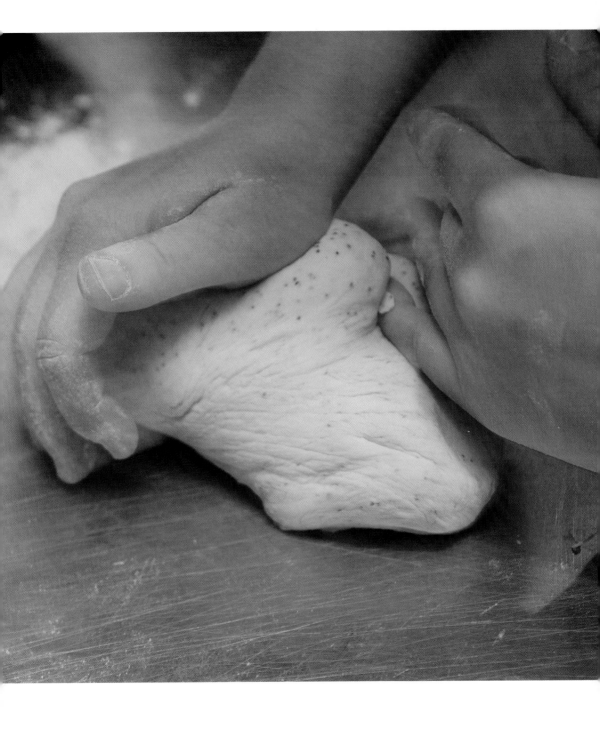

Buttermilk Pancakes

Makes 20 pancakes (never enough)

450 g plain white flour

60 g caster sugar

1 teaspoon bread soda

Pinch of salt

1 free-range egg, beaten

600 ml buttermilk

Mix the dry ingredients together. Make a well in the centre. Using a balloon whisk, mix in the beaten egg. Slowly add the buttermilk and mix until all lumps are gone. This mixture should be a thick batter. Cover with a clean tea towel and allow to rest. (At this stage you can go and buy newspapers!) Heat a heavy-bottomed frying pan and brush with oil. (Be sparing with the oil to avoid greasy pancakes.) Using a large kitchen spoon, drop the batter onto the pan. Allow to cook. You can flip the pancakes when you notice bubbles forming on top. Turn and cook on the other side. Serve with raspberry jam and cream, stewed apple and cream, sliced bananas and maple syrup, stewed berries and vanilla ice cream, Nutella…the list is endless. If you wish, you could also drop blueberries on top of each pancake just after putting them on the pan and before you turn them.

Soup

Beetroot and Apple Soup

Serves 6

90 g butter
2 onions, peeled and diced
2 cloves of garlic, crushed
1 Granny Smith apple, peeled and diced
600 g cooked beetroot, diced
850 ml vegetable stock
300 ml dry cider
Salt and freshly ground white pepper
Crème fraîche, to garnish

Heat a large saucepan. Melt the butter, then add the onions and garlic. Cook until soft, but not coloured. Season. Add the apple and beetroot and coat with the butter. Add the stock and cider and bring to the boil. Reduce the heat and simmer for 10 minutes. Purée the soup in a food processor. Return to the saucepan and reheat. Check seasoning. Serve garnished with crème fraîche.

Apple, Celery and Cider Soup

Serves 6

2 tablespoons sunflower oil
2 onions, finely diced
450 g celery, sliced
1 leek, white part only, diced
1 Granny Smith apple, peeled, cored and chopped
Salt and pepper
2 large potatoes, peeled and chopped
150 ml cider
850 ml vegetable stock
150 ml cream
30 g roasted walnuts

Heat the oil in a large, heavy-based saucepan. Add the onions, celery, leek and apple. Cook without browning. Add seasoning. Add the potato and cook for a further 3 minutes. Add the cider and vegetable stock, bring to the boil and cook for 10 minutes, until the potato is soft. Liquidise until smooth, return to the saucepan and check seasoning. Add cream, reheat – do not boil – and serve with roasted walnuts.

Bacon and Turnip Soup

Serves 6

2 tablespoons sunflower oil
150 g rindless streaky bacon, cut into 1 cm dice
1 onion, peeled and diced
100 g leek, diced
150 g peeled, diced potato
350 g peeled, diced turnip
850 ml chicken stock
100 ml cream
Salt and freshly ground white pepper

Heat a heavy-based saucepan. Add the sunflower oil and heat. Add the bacon and cook until crisp and golden. Remove to a plate using a slotted spoon. Use the bacon fat in the saucepan to brown the onion and leek. Add the potato and turnip and cook for 5 minutes. Season with salt and pepper. Add the chicken stock, bring to the boil and simmer until all the vegetables are soft. Liquidise, return to the saucepan, add the cream and check seasoning. Serve garnished with the crispy bacon.

Roast Onion, Garlic and Cashel Blue Soup

Serves 6

6 onions, peeled and sliced
2 bulbs of garlic
800 ml vegetable stock
Salt and freshly ground white pepper
1 teaspoon picked thyme leaves
30 g butter
300 ml cream
50 g Cashel Blue cheese, grated
2 teaspoons chopped flat-leaf parsley, to garnish
50 g Cashel Blue cheese, grated, to garnish

Preheat the oven to 180°C/350°F/gas 4. Place the onions and garlic in a roasting tray and cover with a third of the stock. Sprinkle with salt, pepper, thyme and butter. Cover with tinfoil and bake in the oven for 1½ hours. Blend in a food processor, pour into a saucepan and add the remaining stock, cream and the cheese. Reheat but do not boil, as the soup may split. Serve garnished with some parsley and the cheese. This is also good with smoked bacon.

King's Broth

Serves 6

A traditional Irish broth that's fit for a king.

60 g butter
1 onion, peeled and finely diced
Salt and freshly ground white pepper
Pinch of powdered mace
225 g leeks, washed and finely diced
225 g peeled potato, finely diced
30 g oatflakes
1.2 litres chicken stock
275 g diced wild salmon
150 ml cream
1 tablespoon chopped flat-leaf parsley, to garnish

Heat a heavy-based saucepan. Add the butter and cook the onion until soft but not brown. Add seasoning and mace. Add the leeks, potato and oatflakes. Cook for 3 minutes. Add the stock and cook for 10 minutes, until the potatoes are soft. Bring to the boil and add the salmon and cream. Do not boil at this stage; simmer for 2 minutes. Serve sprinkled with the chopped parsley.

Nettle Soup

Serves 6

50 g butter
1 onion, peeled and finely chopped
2 leeks, washed and sliced
3 rooster potatoes, peeled and chopped
Salt and pepper
1 litre chicken or vegetable stock
150 g nettle leaves
150 ml cream

Pick young nettles using gloves. Remove the leaves and wash. Heat a large saucepan and melt the butter. Add the onion, leek and potatoes. Toss in the butter until well coated. Season with salt and pepper and cook for 10 minutes, then add stock. Cook until the vegetables are tender. Cool slightly. Place mixture in a liquidiser and blend. Return to the saucepan. Meanwhile, bring a pot of water to boil, add the nettle leaves for 5 seconds, strain through a colander and cool down with ice water to hold their green colour. Squeeze to remove any excess water and chop. Before serving, heat the soup, add cream and nettles to the soup, check seasoning and serve.

Spiced African Soup

Serves 6

2 tablespoons olive oil
1 Spanish onion, finely diced
3 cloves of garlic, finely chopped
1 red pepper, deseeded and finely diced
1 green pepper, deseeded and finely diced
1 red chilli, deseeded and finely diced
Salt and pepper
½ teaspoon chilli flakes
30 g rice
1 tablespoon peanut butter
1.2 litres chicken stock
1 x 400 g tin chopped plum tomatoes
1 cooked chicken breast, shredded
30 g chopped roasted peanuts, to garnish

Heat a large saucepan and add the olive oil. Add all the vegetables and cook slowly, until soft. Add the salt, pepper and chilli flakes to taste. Add the rice and peanut butter and stir well. Then add the chicken stock and tomatoes. Bring to the boil, reduce the heat and simmer for 12 minutes, until the rice is cooked. Check the seasoning and add the shredded cooked chicken. Serve in bowls with chopped peanuts on top.

Sweet Potato, Coconut and Coriander Soup

Serves 6

2 tablespoons sunflower oil
2 onions, finely diced
2 stalks celery, finely diced
1 leek, white part only, finely diced
3 cloves of garlic, finely diced
1 level tablespoon finely chopped ginger
1 red chilli, deseeded and finely chopped
600 g sweet potato, peeled and diced
Salt and pepper
1 litre vegetable stock
250 ml coconut milk
1 tablespoon chopped coriander

Heat the sunflower oil in a large, heavy-based saucepan. Add the onion, celery, leek, garlic, ginger and chilli. Cook slowly, until soft but not coloured. Add the sweet potato and season. Cook for a further 3 minutes. Add the vegetable stock and cook until the sweet potato is soft, about 15 minutes. Liquidise and add the coconut milk. Reheat, check seasoning and add the chopped coriander before serving.

Roast Mushroom Soup with Tarragon

Serves 6

Roasting the mushrooms really brings out the flavour.

700 g flat mushrooms
4 tablespoons sunflower oil
30 g butter
Sprig of thyme
2 onions, finely diced
1 leek, white part only, finely chopped
2 stalks celery, finely chopped
2 cloves of garlic, finely diced
2 potatoes, peeled and chopped
1 litre vegetable stock
Salt and freshly ground white pepper
150 ml cream
1 tablespoon chopped tarragon

Preheat the oven to 220°C/425°F/gas 7. Wipe rather than wash the mushrooms; this holds the flavour. Place in a hot roasting tray. Toss the mushrooms in half the oil and season. Add butter and thyme. Roast for 25 minutes.

Heat the remainder of the sunflower oil in a heavy-based saucepan. Add the onion, leek, celery and garlic. Cook until soft, but do not allow to colour. Add the potatoes and cook for 5 minutes. Add the stock, roasted mushrooms and all the juice from the roasting tray. Bring to the boil and cook until the potatoes are soft. Liquidise until smooth and return to the saucepan. Check the seasoning. Reheat and add the cream and tarragon.

Spiced Chickpea Soup

Serves 6

5 plum tomatoes, cut into quarters
1 aubergine, roughly chopped
1 onion, peeled and chopped
4 cloves of garlic, sliced
1 carrot, peeled and chopped
2 celery stalks, sliced
1 leek, sliced
1 red chilli, finely chopped
1 sprig of thyme
1 sprig of rosemary
Olive oil
Salt and freshly ground white pepper
1½ litres vegetable stock
1 tablespoon rice wine vinegar
1 cup of white wine
1 level teaspoon coriander seeds, toasted and ground
1 level teaspoon mustard seeds, toasted and ground
1 level teaspoon cumin seeds, toasted and ground
2 tablespoons tomato purée
250 g cooked chickpeas
Crème fraîche, to garnish
Chopped coriander, to garnish

Preheat the oven to 200°C/400°F/gas 6. Roast the tomatoes, aubergine, onion, garlic, olive oil, salt and pepper for 40 minutes. In a large saucepan, heat the olive oil and fry off remaining vegetables until tender. Add the herbs and spices and cook for a further 5 minutes. Add the stock, vinegar and wine with the tomato purée and chickpeas. Add all the roasted vegetables and bring to the boil. Simmer for 15 minutes. Blend, check the seasoning and serve with crème fraîche and chopped coriander.

Fish

Gravadlax

Serves 20

Fantastic for a picnic, party, brunch or as an appetiser. Excellent for a large group, as it can be prepared and sliced in advance. Start preparing this 48 hours before you need to serve it.

You will need 2 sides of wild or organic salmon, pin boned and *skin on*. Ask your fishmonger to prepare this for you. (You can also use 1 side of salmon and cut it in half width-wise and use half the marinade.)

For the marinade:

4 shots of vodka   *350 g sugar*
Juice of 2 lemons   *275 g coarse sea salt*
2 tablespoons Dijon mustard   *100 g dill, chopped roughly*
2 tablespoons wholegrain mustard

To serve:

1 bag of dill, chopped finely   *Pickled Cucumber (p. 26)*
2 tablespoons wholegrain mustard *Horseradish Crème Fraîche (p. 34)*
Juice of 2 lemons

Line a tray that is long enough for the salmon with cling film. Place the side of salmon on the cling film, skin side down. In a bowl, mix the vodka, lemon juice, mustards, sugar, salt and dill into a paste. Spread evenly over the flesh of the salmon, making sure all the salmon is covered evenly. Place the other side of salmon, flesh side down, on top of the marinade. This will create a salmon sandwich with the marinade in the middle touching the flesh of both sides. Wrap the salmon tightly in the cling film. This is to hold the marinade in place. Place in the fridge for 48 hours, turning every 8 hours. After 48 hours, remove from the fridge and wash off the marinade. Pat dry with kitchen paper. To serve, mix the dill, mustard and lemon juice together and spread evenly over the flesh. Slice thinly with a sharp knife, as you would smoked salmon. Serve with Pickled Cucumber and Horseradish Crème Fraîche.

Eden's Smokies

Serves 4

This dish, one of my favourites, was on the first menu in Eden. When I changed the menu after 3 months, I took this off. It led to chaos. Two customers walked out, as they had come specifically for Smokies, and I received numerous phone calls. The 'Replace the Smokies' campaign was launched! I learned a valuable lesson – give your customers what they want.

This can be served in individual dishes as a starter, or in a large dish for supper, served with salad and ciabatta. Double the quantity if serving as a main course.

Splash of sunflower oil
500 g naturally smoked haddock, skin off, bones removed and diced
1 punnet of cherry tomatoes, halved
3 spring onions
250 g crème fraîche
Freshly ground white pepper
90 g grated cheddar

Heat a frying pan and add the oil. Fry the smoked haddock on all sides. Add the cherry tomatoes and spring onions. Add the crème fraîche and season with white pepper; you may not need salt, as smoked fish tends to be salty. Bring to the boil and place in one serving dish or individual dishes. Sprinkle with cheddar cheese and brown under the grill.

Tuna Carpaccio

Serves 6

6 tablespoons black peppercorns, crushed
2 tablespoons pink peppercorns, crushed
3 tablespoons brandy
2 tablespoons Dijon mustard
6 tablespoons fresh coriander, leaves chopped
3 tablespoons flat-leaf parsley, chopped
1 tablespoon Maldon sea salt
1 kg tuna centre loin, trimmed
Wasabi, to serve
Watercress, to serve
Crème fraîche, to serve

As this is being served raw, the tuna must be really fresh. Heat a dry frying pan and toss the crushed peppercorns in the pan for 1 minute to release the flavour. Remove from the pan and cool. Mix the brandy and mustard together and rub the mix over all sides of the tuna. On a flat tray, mix the herbs and salt together. Roll the tuna in the mix, ensuring that all sides of the tuna are well covered. Wrap in cling film and place in the freezer for 30 minutes, then remove and place in the fridge for 4 hours. Just before serving, remove cling film and slice as thinly as possible with a very sharp knife. Serve with wasabi (Japanese horseradish, available in Asian markets), watercress and crème fraîche.

Ceviche

Serves 6 as a starter

1 kg lemon sole, skin off
1 handful chopped coriander leaves
Juice of 3 limes
4 lime leaves
300 ml rice wine vinegar
1 stick lemongrass, cut into 3 chunks and flattened to release flavour
1 red chilli, finely sliced
5 white peppercorns
Pickled Cucumber (p. 26), to serve
Lime wedges, to serve

The fish must be very fresh. Cut the fish into strips about 2½ cm wide, the length of the fish fillet. Place on a flat plastic tray and sprinkle with the chopped coriander.

In a saucepan, heat all the other ingredients. Bring to the boil to infuse the flavours. Remove from the heat and **cool completely** (if it is not cold, it will toughen the fish). Pour over the fish, cover with cling film and refrigerate for 6 hours. Remove from the marinade. Serve with Pickled Cucumber and a lime wedge.

Oysters with Bloody Mary Granita

Serves 6

For the granita:

300 ml good-quality tomato juice

Juice of 1 lime

5 g caster sugar

1 shot of vodka

2 teaspoons Worcestershire sauce

1 teaspoon Tabasco

Allow 6 oysters per person (or an unending supply, if you are in my house!).
Mix all the ingredients for the granita together in a bowl. Stir to dissolve the
sugar. Place in a plastic tray and put in the freezer. Remove from the freezer
every hour to mix well with a balloon whisk. It will take about 4 hours to
freeze. Open the oysters and loosen the flesh from the shell. Do not serve
oysters if the shell is open, if they look very dry or if they smell off. Place
crushed ice or seaweed on a plate, then place oysters on the plate. The
granita looks great in shot glasses placed in the centre of the dish.

Cajun Mackerel with Lime Aioli

Serves 4

This is an excellent starter or light supper dish.

Allow 1 butterfly fillet of mackerel per person

1 tablespoon Cajun spices

100 g flour

1 tablespoon olive oil

1 tablespoon butter

Lime Wedges to serve

Aioli (p. 6) or Mango Salsa (p. 132), to serve

Mix the Cajun seasoning with the flour. Toss the mackerel fillets in the flour,
making sure they are evenly covered. Shake off excess flour. Heat a frying
pan and add the oil. Place mackerel fillets in the oil, flesh side down. Cook for
2 minutes and turn. Add the butter to the pan and allow to foam. Cook for a
further 2 minutes, remove from the pan and drain. Serve on warm plates with
a wedge of lime and Aioli or Mango Salsa.

Brown Shrimp and Crab Salad

Serves 4

300 g crab meat, picked through to remove any shell
100 g brown shrimp
1 tablespoon coriander leaves, chopped
Juice of 1 lemon
Salt and freshly ground white pepper
½ teaspoon curry powder
2 tablespoons Aioli (p. 6)
Shiso cress, to garnish
Sliced cucumber, to garnish
Toast or Guinness Bread (p. 41), to serve

Place crab meat in a bowl and flake with a fork. Watch out for shell or cartilage and remove any bits carefully. Mix in the shrimp, coriander and lemon juice. Season. In another bowl, mix the curry powder and Aioli together. Add to the crab mix. Spoon onto a serving plate, or use a pastry/tian ring to give a more formal, round shape. Garnish with cress and cucumber. Serve with toast or Guinness Bread.

Seared Tuna Steak with Cannellini Bean Salad and Salsa Verde

Serves 4

Allow 1 x 200 g tuna steak per person. This should be thickly cut to enable you to serve the tuna rare.

For the salad:
100 g cannellini beans, soaked in cold water overnight
100 g frozen garden peas or sugar snaps, cooked and cooled
2 plum tomatoes, diced
100 g rocket leaves
50 g stoned kalamata olives
2 tablespoons extra virgin olive oil
1 tablespoon balsamic vinegar
100 g crumbled feta cheese (optional)
Salt and freshly ground white pepper
Salsa Verde (p. 29), to serve
Lemon wedges, to serve

Drain off cannellini beans and rinse in cold water. Place in a saucepan, cover with cold water and cook until tender. Drain and cool. Just prior to serving, gently mix the remaining ingredients for the salad together and season. Divide between serving plates. Brush the tuna steaks with a little olive oil. Season with salt and pepper. Heat a griddle pan until you see a blue haze rising from the pan. Sear the tuna on both sides for 15 seconds. This will seal the outside but keep the inside rare. If you wish to serve the tuna more cooked, leave it on the pan for longer. Be careful, as the tuna will dry out quite quickly. To serve, place the seared tuna on the salad and garnish with Salsa Verde and a lemon wedge.

Pan-fried Halibut Served with Braised Fennel and Chervil Beurre Blanc

Serves 4

This sauce and garnish works well with most white fish.

Allow 180 g halibut per person, skin left on
1 tablespoon olive oil
1 tablespoon butter
Salt and freshly ground white pepper
Braised Fennel (p. 151)
New potatoes or Mashed Potato (p. 168), to serve

For the sauce:
1 tablespoon olive oil
2 shallots, peeled and finely diced
1 bay leaf
Zest and juice of 1 lemon
3 tablespoons white wine
75 ml cream
200 g cold butter, diced and kept in fridge
2 tablespoons finely diced tomato
1 tablespoon chopped chervil

To make the sauce, heat the oil in a saucepan. Add the shallots and cook over a low heat until soft but not brown. Add the bay leaf, lemon juice, zest and white wine. Increase the heat and reduce the liquid volume by half. Add the cream and reduce by half again. Remove the pan from the heat and, using a balloon whisk, add the butter, one cube at a time. When all the butter has been whisked in, add the tomato and chervil. Covered with cling film, this sauce will hold for 1 hour. To cook the fish, heat a frying pan and add the oil. Season the fish and place in the frying pan, skin side down. Cook for 4 minutes. Add the butter and allow to foam, then turn the fish and cook for a further 2 minutes. When cooked, the fish will be firm to touch and bounce back when pressed. To serve, divide the Braised Fennel between 4 plates. Place the fish on top, skin side up, and drizzle with sauce. Serve with new potatoes or mash.

Pan-fried Salmon with Balsamic Roast Beetroot and Horseradish Crème Fraîche

Serves 4

This dish is excellent using wild salmon. You can also use organic salmon, hake or Pollock.

Allow 180 g fish per person
1 tablespoon olive oil
1 tablespoon butter
Salt and freshly ground white pepper
1 x Horseradish Crème Fraîche (p. 34)
100 g rocket leaves, to garnish

For the beetroot:
4 whole raw beetroot, or for convenience use vacuum-packed whole beetroot
1 tablespoon olive oil
2 tablespoons balsamic vinegar
Salt and freshly ground black pepper

To prepare the beetroot, preheat the oven to 200°C/400°F/gas 6. If using raw beetroot, place clean, unpeeled beets in cold water. Bring to the boil and simmer for 30 minutes until tender. Cool under cold water. Peel using a sharp knife; make sure you wear plastic gloves. Cut the beetroot into 6 wedges. Toss in the oil, vinegar and seasoning, place on a baking tray and roast for 20 minutes. To cook the fish, heat a frying pan and add the oil. Carefully place the seasoned fish in the pan. Cook for 3 minutes. Add the butter and allow to foam. Turn fish and cook for a further 2 minutes. To serve, divide the beetroot between 4 plates. Place the fish on top and place a dollop of Horseradish Crème Fraîche on each piece of fish and garnish with rocket leaves.

Roast Pollock with Chorizo, Almonds and Baby Spinach

Serves 4

Butter
Olive oil
Allow 1 x 200 g Pollock cutlet per person
180 g chorizo sausage, finely chopped
120 g toasted flaked almonds
200 g baby spinach

Preheat the oven to 190°C/375°F/gas 5. Heat a frying pan. Add the butter and a little olive oil. Brown the fish cutlets on both sides and place in a greased ovenproof dish. Bake for 7 minutes, until the flesh comes away from the bone. Meanwhile, add the chorizo to the frying pan and sauté until crisp. Add the almonds and finally the baby spinach. Serve the Pollock on a warm dish with a spoon of the spinach and chorizo mix on each plate. Serve with new potatoes and salad.

Pan-seared Scallops with Pea and Mint Risotto

Serves 4

It helps to have an able assistant on standby to help you plate this dish, otherwise the scallops will be overcooked.

Allow 5 or 6 king scallops per person
1 tablespoon olive oil
1 tablespoon butter
Salt and freshly ground white pepper

For the risotto:
1 x basic risotto recipe (p. 163)
100 g cooked garden peas
Juice of 1 lemon
1 tablespoon chopped fresh mint

To garnish:
8 thin slices of pancetta, optional (pancetta is a cured Italian ham that adds a wonderful flavour to the dish).

Follow the risotto recipe on p. 163. Before serving, add the peas, lemon juice and mint. Prepare the scallops by removing the orange coral from scallop. This is held in place by sinew which toughens when cooked, so cut it away. Heat a large frying pan and add the olive oil. Cook the sliced pancetta on both sides until crisp. Remove the pancetta from the pan and drain on kitchen paper. Keep warm. Have the risotto ready to serve now, as this dish needs to be served immediately. Season scallops and place in the pan. The fat from the pancetta will give a lovely flavour. Cook the scallops in 2 batches, as they will overcook very quickly. They only take about 40 seconds to cook on each side. When cooked, add the butter and the orange coral and allow the butter to foam. To serve, place risotto in the centre of a warm plate, arrange the scallops around the risotto and pour the butter and juices from the pan over the scallops. Place the pancetta on top of the risotto and enjoy.

Grilled Swordfish Served with Black Bean Salsa and Guacamole

Serves 4

Allow 1 x 200 g swordfish steak per person, at least 1 inch thick
Black Bean Salsa (p. 8)
Avocado slices, to garnish
Lime slices, to garnish

For the marinade:
2 cloves of garlic, crushed
Juice of 1 lemon
2 tablespoons olive oil
1 tablespoon soy sauce
½ red chilli, deseeded and diced

For the guacamole:
2 Hass avocados, peeled and diced finely (if the avocados are very soft, you can mash them)
1 clove of garlic, crushed
Juice of 2 limes
1 red chilli, deseeded and finely diced
3 tablespoons chopped fresh coriander
Salt and freshly ground white pepper

To make the marinade, mix all the marinade ingredients together and pour over the fish steaks 1 hour before cooking. Do not leave for longer, or the texture of the fish will start to break down. To make the guacamole, mix all the ingredients together in a bowl. Immediately before serving, heat a griddle pan until a blue haze appears. Drain the marinade from the fish. Sear the swordfish steaks for 1 minute on each side. Cook for longer if you do not want the fish to be rare. Serve the fish on Black Bean Salsa. Garnish with avocado and a slice of lime.

Baked Fish Parcels

Serves 4

An excellent dish for dinner parties, as the parcels can be prepared in advance and held in the fridge for 4 hours before being cooked.

Allow 200 g of white fish per person (we use plaice, sole or John Dory fillets)
2 tablespoons olive oil
100 g baby spinach
2 small bulbs of fennel, shaved
Salt and freshly ground white pepper
4 tablespoons white wine
2 cloves of garlic, sliced
1 punnet cherry tomatoes, halved
4 tablespoons Salsa Verde (p. 29)
Parchment paper and twine to tie

Preheat the oven to 200°C/400°F/gas 6. Cut 4 circles of parchment paper about 35 cm in diameter. Lay out on work top. Brush the middle of the paper with olive oil. Divide the spinach and fennel between the parcels. Place the fish on top, sprinkle with salt and pepper and the white wine. Cover with the garlic and cherry tomatoes. Add 1 tablespoon of Salsa Verde to each piece of fish. Gather the edges of the paper into an alms purse and tie with heat-proof twine. Bake for 8 to 12 minutes. The cooking time will depend on the thickness of the fish. Serve the fish on a plate in the parcel, allowing guests to open the parcel to reveal the fish inside. Serve with salad and new potatoes.

Steamed Mussels in a Coconut and Saffron Broth

Serves 4

1 kg mussels in shell
100 ml white wine
1 bulb of fennel, shaved

1 red chilli, deseeded and finely sliced
Coriander sprigs

For the broth:
500 g white fish bones
2 bulbs of fennel
1 carrot, diced
2 stalks of celery, sliced
1 white onion, peeled and chopped
1 head of garlic, cut in half

4 bay leaves
1 leek, chopped
2 sticks of lemongrass
5 white peppercorns
1½ litres water

To finish the broth:
1 x 400 g tin coconut milk
Juice of half a lime

Pinch of saffron
Salt and pepper

Wash the fish bones and place in a heavy-based saucepan with all the broth ingredients. Cover with the water, bring to the boil and skim off any froth. Reduce the heat and cook for 30 minutes. Remove from the heat and pour through a very fine sieve. Discard all the bones and vegetables. Keep the liquid and return to the saucepan. Add the coconut milk, lime juice, saffron and seasoning. Rinse the mussels and remove the beards. Throw away any that remain open. Heat a saucepan large enough for all the mussels. When hot, add the mussels in their shells and the white wine. Cover and shake. Check after 5 minutes; the mussels should be open. If not, cover for a further 3 minutes. Reheat the fish broth. Divide the mussels into 6 soup bowls and cover with the broth. Garnish with the shaved fennel, chilli and coriander.

Roast Whole Sea Bass/Sea Bream

Serves 4

Allow 1 whole fish per person, average weight 450 g. Ask your fishmonger to gut, descale and remove the head from each fish.
Salt and freshly ground pepper
Juice and zest of 1 lemon
1 tablespoon olive oil
1 tablespoon white wine
1 tablespoon chopped parsley

Mix all the ingredients together and rub on the fish. Place in the fridge for at least 1 hour. Preheat the oven to 200°C/400°F/gas 6.

Heat a roasting tray on the stove. Add 2 tablespoons of oil. When a blue haze rises from the roasting tray, place the fish in the tray. Seal both sides of the fish until golden brown and place in the oven. Cook until the flesh is springy, about 10 minutes.

This is where the Larder section comes into play: I would serve the fish with Tabbouleh (p. 157) or Couscous (p. 154) and use Pickled Chilli (p. 11), Tapenade (p. 31), Salsa Verde (p. 29) or Peperonata (p. 24) as a garnish.

Fillet of Turbot Served with Clam and Butterbean Cassoulet

Serves 4

This cassoulet can be used as a garnish for most fillets of fish.

Allow 1 x 180 g skinless fillet of fish per person
500 g clams   *1 x 400 g tin cooked butterbeans*
200 ml coconut milk   *1 teaspoon chopped coriander, to garnish*
100 g baby spinach

For the cooking liqueur:
2 shallots, finely chopped   *½ red chilli, deseeded and chopped*
100 ml dry white wine   *1 lime, cut into wedges*
2 bay leaves   *1 teaspoon chopped fresh ginger*
2 cloves of garlic, sliced

Wash the clams in cold water. Place all the ingredients for the cooking liqueur in a large, flat ovenproof saucepan or casserole dish. Place over a medium heat and cover tightly. Bring to the boil. Add the clams and shake well. Add the coconut milk and butterbeans and bring to the boil. Gently place the spinach and fish on top. Cover and cook for approximately 10 to 12 minutes. When cooked, the fish will be springy but not soft to touch. Garnish with chopped coriander and serve.

Meat

Beef Carpaccio

Serves 6 as an appetiser

When buying beef, always buy beef that has been hung for at least 20 days. This allows the flavour to develop and the meat to become tender.

15 g cumin seeds
15 g coriander seeds
15 g fennel seeds
15 g black peppercorns
500 g fillet of beef, in one piece

For the dipping sauce:
1 tablespoon soy sauce
¼ teaspoon sugar
1 tablespoon rice wine vinegar
Juice of 1 lime
¼ teaspoon fresh ginger, chopped
½ red chilli finely diced
Rocket leaves, to garnish
Extra virgin olive oil, to garnish
Shaved Parmesan cheese, to garnish

Toast the cumin, coriander, fennel and peppercorns on a hot, dry pan to bring out the flavour. Grind in a pestle and mortar or spice grinder. Rub the ground spices into the fillet of beef. Heat a frying pan and seal the fillet all the way around. Remove from the pan and allow to cool. Wrap in cling film and put in the freezer for 90 minutes, until it is firm to touch. To make the dipping sauce, mix all the ingredients together. To serve, slice the beef very thinly with a sharp knife. Serve with the dipping sauce in a ramekin and garnish with rocket leaves, a drizzle of olive oil and shaved Parmesan.

Parma Ham Served with Goat's Cheese, Baked Figs, Wild Honey and Toasted Hazelnuts

Serves 6

6 ripe figs
3 crottin of St Tola goat's cheese, split in half around the centre
2 tablespoons wild honey
6 slices Parma ham
Rocket leaves, to garnish
30 g chopped toasted hazelnuts, skin off, to garnish

Preheat the oven to 190°C/375°F/gas 5. Cut figs in quarters, almost to the base. If you keep them intact at the base, they will open like a flower. Place on a baking sheet. Place the goat's cheese on top of the figs and drizzle with honey. Bake for 5 to 7 minutes, until the cheese is brown. Meanwhile, fold the Parma ham into a roll. Remove the figs from the oven and place on individual plates. Place the Parma ham on top of each fig and garnish with the rocket leaves and toasted hazelnuts.

Filo Baskets with Black Pudding and Cashel Blue Cheese

These are an excellent appetiser or supper dish.

90 g black pudding, cut into 1 cm slices and casing removed
Butter
1 filo basket (p. 208) (as these are savoury baskets, use flour on the work top)
1 tablespoon Onion Marmalade (p. 20)
40 g Cashel Blue cheese, grated
Balsamic Reduction (p. 16), to garnish

Preheat the oven to 190°C/375°F/gas 5. Heat a frying pan and cook the black pudding in butter for 5 minutes. Place the filo baskets on a baking sheet. Place 1 tablespoon of Onion Marmalade in the base of the basket. Place the black pudding into the baskets and place the grated cheese on top. Bake for 12 minutes, until the cheese is melted. Serve on warm plates garnished with the reduced balsamic vinegar.

Seared Lamb's Kidneys with Lyonnaise Potatoes and Wholegrain Mustard Jus

Serves 4

8 kidneys
200 ml milk
12 cooked new potatoes, skin on
2 shallots
1 teaspoon sunflower oil
1 teaspoon butter
Splash of Marsala
2 tablespoons wholegrain mustard
200 ml jus (p. 31)

Halve the kidneys and remove the outer skin and white sinew in the core. Soak in milk for 10 minutes. For the Lyonnaise potatoes, slice the new potatoes and shallots. Heat a frying pan. Add the oil and butter and sauté the shallots until soft. Add the sliced potatoes and cook until golden brown. Keep warm. Preheat another frying pan and lightly oil. Season and sear the kidneys in the pan for 30 seconds on each side. They should be soft to touch and pink in the centre. Remove to a hot plate. Add a splash of Marsala to the kidney pan and bring to the boil. Add the mustard and stir in the jus. Heat through. To serve, place the potatoes in the centre of the plate, place the kidneys on top and spoon the jus over.

Braised Lamb Shank

Serves 6

Allow 1 lamb shank per person. Start this recipe 1 or 2 days before you plan to serve it.

For the marinade:
6 cloves of garlic, chopped
3 tablespoons olive oil
6 tablespoons red wine
2 sprigs rosemary, picked and chopped
1 lemon, sliced

To cook 6 shanks:
2 tablespoons olive oil
1 onion, diced
2 carrots, diced
2 stalks celery, diced
100 g tomato purée
1½ litres chicken or vegetable stock
Sprig of rosemary

To make the marinade, combine all the ingredients for the marinade. Rub into the shanks and place in a container. Cover and keep in the fridge. Preheat the oven to 200°C/400°F/gas 6. Remove the shanks from the marinade and pat dry. Heat a frying pan with olive oil. Add the shanks and brown on all sides. Remove and place in a deep ovenproof dish. Fry the vegetables until golden brown. Add the purée and stock and bring to the boil. Pour over the shanks, cover tightly with tinfoil and place in the oven. Cook for 2 hours, until the meat is tender and ready to fall off the bone. Serve with Mashed Potato (p. 168) and roast carrots and parsnips (p. 161).

I love to serve this dish with barley instead of Mashed Potato. If you wish to do this, rinse 200 g pearl barley in cold water. Add it to the shanks in the oven after 1 hour. It will cook in the stock and will absorb the lamb flavours.

Roast Magret of Duck with Dauphinoise Potatoes and Rhubarb Balsamic Jus

Serves 4

2 x 400 g duck breasts
Dauphinoise Potatoes (p. 172)

Salt and freshly ground black pepper

For the sauce:
2 young, thin stalks of rhubarb
1 tablespoon water
1 tablespoon sugar

2 tablespoons balsamic vinegar
200 ml jus (p. 31)
Salt and freshly ground pepper

For the game chips:
2 sweet potatoes, peeled and thinly sliced (you need to use a mandolin for this to get the slices paper thin)

Cut the rhubarb into 3 cm lengths and place in a saucepan. Add the water and sugar, cover and cook slowly until tender but still holding its shape. Strain carefully, leaving the rhubarb in the saucepan. Add the balsamic vinegar to the pot and reduce by half; this will allow the vinegar to coat the rhubarb. Add the jus and bring to the boil. Season. For the game chips, heat a deep-fat fryer to 160°C/320°F. Deep fry the sweet potato slices in small batches, until fully crisp. Drain on kitchen paper. If these are not crisp enough, dry out in the oven for a further 10 minutes. These will hold overnight in an airtight container.

To cook the duck, preheat the oven to 200°C/400°F/gas 6. Score the fat on the duck at ½ cm intervals in a criss-cross fashion. Season well. Heat a frying pan and place the duck breasts in the pan, fat side down. Do not turn until the fat is golden brown and crispy, then turn and lightly brown the flesh side. Remove from the pan carefully, as duck fat will splash and burn you badly. Place on a roasting tray and place in the oven for 8 minutes; this will take less time if you have a fan oven. Remove from the oven and cover with tinfoil and keep in a warm place. The duck, like all meat, must rest before you carve it, otherwise it will be tough. To serve, heat the Dauphinoise Potatoes (p. 172) and divide between 4 plates. Carve the duck breasts into thin slices using a sharp knife. Place on top of the potato and spoon sauce over it. Garnish with crisp game chips.

Kumquat Jus

Serves 4

Another excellent sauce with duck as an alternative to rhubarb jus.

Bring 200 ml jus (p. 31) to the boil. Add 4 tablespoons Kumquat Relish (p. 19) to jus and serve.

Wild Boar Stew

Serves 6

Start this stew a day or two before you plan to serve it. I believe all stews taste better on the second or third day. However, if this is the case, you must cool the stew down quickly and store it in the fridge when it is totally cold. When you are reheating it, it must be heated through. Bring to the boil and simmer for 10 minutes, stirring occasionally.

1 kg diced wild boar or pork
Olive oil, for frying
225 g diced onion
225 g diced carrot
225 g diced celery
200 ml Armagnac or brandy
1½ litres jus (p. 31)
200 g prunes soaked in 50 ml Armagnac or brandy (I use apricots instead if I am making this stew with pork)
Mashed Potato (p. 168), to serve

For the marinade:
4 cloves of garlic
1 tablespoon paprika
2 sprigs thyme
1 sprig rosemary
1 tablespoon sunflower oil

To make the marinade, mix all the ingredients together. Toss the meat in the marinade, cover and leave in the fridge overnight. To cook, preheat the oven to 200°C/400°F/gas 6. Heat a frying pan, add the olive oil and brown the meat on all sides. Transfer to an ovenproof dish. Fry the onions, carrots and celery in the frying pan. Add the Armagnac or brandy. Bring to the boil, then add the jus. Bring to the boil again and pour over the meat. Cover tightly with tinfoil and place in the oven for 90 minutes. Before serving, add prunes or apricots and reheat for 5 minutes. Serve with Mashed Potato (p. 168).

Sausages Served with Swede and Smoked Bacon Cake with Cider Jus

Serves 4

The range of gourmet sausages out there is endless, so get yourself to your local butcher or farmers' market and treat yourself to Hick's sausages. We use venison sausages, wild boar and apple, duck and fennel.

Allow 2 sausages per person

For the Swede Cakes:

300 g peeled and diced turnip
Knob of butter
4 slices smoked streaky bacon,
cut into strips and cooked until crispy

150 g Mashed Potato (p. 168)
2 spring onions, finely chopped
50 g grated Parmesan
Salt and freshly ground white pepper

For the sauce:

100 ml cider
2 Granny Smith apples, cored and cut into eighths
200 ml jus (p. 31)

Place the diced turnip in a saucepan and add a knob of butter, salt and white pepper. Cover with water and bring to the boil. Reduce the heat and cook until tender. Drain and mash using a potato masher. Cool.

Mix all the remaining ingredients for the Swede Cakes together in a bowl. Check the seasoning. Shake some flour on a work surface. Shape the cake mix into 8 little cakes. Heat a frying pan, add 1 tablespoon of olive oil and fry the cakes until golden brown. Drain on kitchen paper and keep warm.

For the sauce, heat a saucepan and bring the cider to the boil. Add the apple wedges and cook until soft, but still holding their shape. Add jus and heat. Check seasoning. Cook the sausages in a pan with a little oil or lard for flavour. Brown on all sides and then cover and reduce the heat. The sausages will cook slowly and retain their moisture in this way. This will take about 20 minutes, depending on the thickness. To serve, place the Swede Cakes on a warm plate and place sausages on top. Spoon sauce over sausages. These are also excellent with Roast Root Vegetables (p. 161).

Pan-fried Fillet of Venison Served with Rosti Potato, Blue Cheese, Fennel, Pear and Walnut Salad and Red Wine Jus

Serves 4

For the meat:
Allow 1 x 180 g fillet of venison per person
Olive oil, for frying
Salt and freshly ground black pepper
3 tablespoons red wine
200 ml jus (p. 31)
1 teaspoon picked thyme leaves

For the Rosti Potatoes:
Allow 1 large potato per person
Duck fat to cook (if not available, use a mixture of clarified butter and oil)
Salt and freshly ground white pepper

For the salad:
150 g crumbled Cashel Blue cheese
2 bulbs of fennel, sliced thinly
2 pears, peeled, core removed and cut into eighths
100 g rocket leaves
50 g toasted walnuts
Freshly ground black pepper
Extra virgin olive oil
Balsamic vinegar

Peel and grate the potato into a tea towel, season and squeeze to remove any excess liquid. Heat a large frying pan and add 4 tablespoons of duck fat to the pan. Carefully place 4 tian rings in the pan. Using a spoon, place the grated potato in each tian ring and push down until solid. Each should be about 1 cm high. Cook until golden brown and flip over to finish cooking. Remove from the pan, drain on kitchen paper and keep warm until ready to serve.

For the salad, mix all the ingredients together and drizzle with the oil and vinegar just before serving.

To cook the venison, preheat the oven to 200°C/400°F/gas 6. Heat a frying pan with an ovenproof handle. Add the oil to the pan and heat until shimmering and hot. Season the venison fillets and place in the pan. Seal on all sides until brown. Place in the oven for 8 to 10 minutes. Remove from the oven, take the meat out of the pan, cover with tinfoil and keep warm. This is essential to allow the meat to rest and remain tender. Return the frying pan to the heat and add the red wine. Reduce to a syrup and then add the jus and thyme. Check seasoning.

To serve, dress the salad and place on a plate. Put the Rosti Potato on the plate and place the venison fillet on top. Pour the sauce over and garnish with a sprig of fresh thyme. More traditionally, you could serve the venison with Roast Root Vegetables (p. 161) or Ratatouille (p. 147) instead of the salad.

Pan-fried Beef with Chips and Béarnaise

Serves 4

The beef argument: what cut to serve? I think sirloin has more flavour, fillet is more tender. However, now that t-bone is back on the menu, this is my favourite, as you get the best of both and the flavour from the bone. The choice is yours. Again, ensure the beef has been hung for at least 20 days. Build up a good relationship with your butcher, it will serve you well.

Allow 1 red onion per person
Olive oil
Salt and pepper
Balsamic vinegar
Allow 2 Maris Piper potatoes per person
Allow 1 x 240 g fillet or sirloin of beef per person
Allow 60 g Béarnaise Sauce per person (p. 6)

To roast the onions, preheat the oven to 200°C/400°F/gas 6. Peel the red onions and cut in quarters down to the root. Toss in olive oil, salt, pepper and balsamic vinegar. Place on a roasting tray in the preheated oven for 15 minutes. Peel and wash the potatoes. Cut into chips using a sharp knife or mandolin. Dry with kitchen paper. In a deep-sided saucepan or deep-fat fryer, heat the oil to 180°C/350°F. Cook chips and season. You can also par-cook the chips in oil at 130°C/265°F. This will allow you to cook the chips in advance if cooking for a large group. To do this, cook the chips in advance at 130°C/265°F, remove and drain on greaseproof paper. Before serving, turn the heat of the fryer up to 180°C/350°F and brown the chips quickly.

To cook the steak, heat a griddle pan until smoking. Brush with olive oil, season the steaks and place on the pan. Brown on all sides. If you are serving the steak more cooked than medium-rare, it is easier to finish cooking them in the oven, as your kitchen will be less smoky and the outside of the steak will not blacken.

To serve, place the chips and steak on a warm plate, put the onions on top of the steak and smother with Béarnaise Sauce.

Roast Fillet of Beef Served with Roast Tomatoes, Garlic, Rocket, Parmesan and Onion Marmalade

Serves 4

2 tablespoons finely grated Parmesan
4 tablespoons mixed crushed peppercorns (green, black, white and pink)
1 kg fillet of beef
2 heads of garlic, cut in half
8 tomatoes on the vine
2 tablespoons olive oil

To serve:
100 g rocket
Extra virgin olive oil
Balsamic vinegar
50 g shaved Parmesan
1 x Onion Marmalade (p. 20)

Preheat the oven to 200°C/400°F/gas 6.

Mix the Parmesan and crushed peppercorns together. Roll the fillet of beef in the mix, covering evenly. Place the garlic and tomatoes in an ovenproof dish, season and drizzle with olive oil. Roast in the oven for 20 minutes.

Heat a large frying pan and add olive oil. Place the beef in the pan and sear the outside of the beef. Place in the oven and cook for 20 minutes. Remove from the oven, cover with tinfoil and allow to rest in a warm place for 10 minutes. Dress the rocket with olive oil and balsamic vinegar. Arrange the rocket on a large platter. Carve the beef with a sharp knife. Arrange the sliced beef on the rocket. Garnish with shaved Parmesan. Serve with the roast tomatoes, Onion Marmalade and crusty bread. My favourite dinner.

Lamb Tagine served with Couscous and Tzatziki

Serves 6

Start this dish 1 day before you are going to serve it.

1 kg diced lamb or hogget (neck and shoulder are good for this dish)

225 g onion, diced

225 g carrot, diced

225 g celery, diced

1 x 400 g tin chopped tomatoes

1 litre jus (p. 31)

2 sprigs rosemary

1 sprig thyme

Salt and freshly ground white pepper

Chopped parsley, to garnish

40 g toasted flaked almonds, to garnish

Couscous (p. 154), to serve

Tzatziki (p. 34), to serve

For the marinade:

1 tablespoon paprika

1 tablespoon cumin seeds

1 tablespoon coriander seeds

8 cloves of garlic, sliced

1 cinnamon stick

1 tablespoon wholegrain mustard

500 ml red wine

Mix all the ingredients for the marinade together. Coat the lamb with the mixture and place in a container in the fridge for 24 hours.

To cook, preheat the oven to 190°C/375°F/gas 5. Remove the lamb from the marinade. Heat a frying pan, season the lamb and fry until brown. Place in an ovenproof dish. Put the onion, carrot and celery in the pan and brown. Add the tomatoes, jus and herbs to the frying pan. Bring to the boil. Pour over the lamb and cover tightly with tinfoil. Place in the oven and cook for 90 minutes. Serve with Couscous, Tzatziki and garnish with chopped parsley and toasted flaked almonds.

Irish Stew

Serves 4

You can also make this stew with neck of lamb. Allow 1 neck per person and ask your butcher to cut it into 1½ cm slices for you. The stew will be bony but the flavour is fantastic.

750 g diced lamb or hogget
1½ litres chicken stock or water
2 sprigs thyme
Salt and freshly ground white pepper
4 white onions, peeled and diced
225 g carrot, diced
225 g leek, diced
225 g celery, diced
225 g potato, diced
Chopped parsley, to garnish

Place the meat in a saucepan and cover with cold water. Bring to the boil and skim. Drain and cover again with the chicken stock or cold water. Add thyme and seasoning. Bring to the boil, skim off any froth and then simmer for 1 hour. Add the diced vegetables and cook for about 30 minutes, until tender. Correct the seasoning and serve with chopped parsley.

Herb-Crusted Rack of Spring Lamb with Tomato Basil Jus

Serves 4

For a real treat, get some Blasket Island lamb from Gerry Kennedy's butcher shop in Dingle.

For the herb-crusted lamb:
Allow 3 or 4 chops of lamb on each rack per person (for 4 people you will need 2 racks with 6 to 8 chops in each)
1 tablespoon sunflower oil
2 cloves of garlic, crushed
100 g breadcrumbs
Salt and freshly ground white pepper
1 tablespoon chopped parsley
1 tablespoon chopped rosemary
2 tablespoons Dijon or wholegrain mustard
Mashed Potato (p. 168), to serve

For the sauce:
Splash of red wine
250 ml jus (p. 31)
1 tomato, deseeded and diced
1 tablespoon basil, chopped

For the crispy aubergine slices to garnish:
1 aubergine, cut into 1 cm circles
Salt
50 ml olive oil

Preheat the oven to 190°C/375°F/gas 5. Mix the oil with the garlic. Add the breadcrumbs and mix well. Season. Place on a roasting tray and put in the oven for 15 minutes, tossing every 5 minutes to get an even golden-brown colour. Remove from the oven, cool and add the herbs. Increase the heat of the oven to 200°C/400°F/gas 6.

To make the crispy aubergine slices, heat the oven to 200°C/400°F/gas 6.

Sprinkle the salt on the aubergine flesh. Leave for 20 minutes. Pat dry with kitchen paper. Brush both sides with oil, lay on a baking tin and put in the oven for 12 to 15 minutes.

Trim the racks of lamb and score the fat with a sharp knife; you can also ask your butcher to do this for you. Heat a frying pan and season the racks with salt and freshly ground white pepper. Seal in the pan until golden brown on all sides. Place in the oven and cook for 10 to 15 minutes, depending on how pink you like to eat your lamb. Remove from the oven, brush with mustard and sprinkle the crust onto the rack. Cover with tinfoil and keep in a warm place for at least 10 minutes. The meat must rest before you serve it.

To make the sauce, once the lamb is removed from the frying pan. Drain off grease and add a splash of red wine. Bring to the boil, then add the jus. Check the seasoning. Just before serving, add the tomato and basil.

To serve, place the mash on a hot plate. Slice each rack into chops, using the bone as a guide. Arrange on mash and spoon the sauce over the meat. Garnish with aubergine slices.

Confit of Duck Leg

Serves 6

Confit comes from the French term 'to preserve'. The duck leg is marinated overnight with salt and herbs, brushed dry and slowly cooked in duck fat. It is cooled in the fat and stored in the fat until ready to reheat and eat.

6 large male duck legs (ask your butcher to remove the knuckle bone from each one)
3 teaspoons coarse sea salt
2 sprigs rosemary, chopped
2 sprigs thyme, chopped
1½ kg duck fat (you may have to ask your butcher to order this for you)
6 cloves of garlic
2 star anise
1 orange, skin on, cut into wedges
10 black peppercorns
1 teaspoon fennel seeds
Lentils du Puy (p. 169), to serve

Mix the salt, rosemary and thyme together and rub into the flesh of the duck legs. Place on a tray, cover and place in the fridge overnight. To cook, preheat the oven to 180°C/350°F/gas 4. Remove the duck legs from the fridge and wipe off the salt and herbs. Place in a deep ovenproof dish. Heat the duck fat and add all the other ingredients. Pour over the duck legs. Cover tightly with tinfoil and place in the oven. Cook for 2½ hours. This must be cooked slowly. You will know duck legs are cooked when the bone is loose in the leg. Remove from the oven and cool the duck legs in the fat. Stored in fat, this will keep for 1 week in the fridge.

To serve, heat a frying pan. Remove the duck legs from the fat, place in the pan skin side down and reheat in the oven for 15 minutes. Do not turn; this will make the skin nice and crispy. We serve Confit of Duck with a salad and Lentils du Puy (p. 169). Melt the duck fat and strain through a sieve. Keep in an airtight container in the fridge; you can reuse this fat.

Breast of Chicken Tandoori with Bombay Potatoes

Serves 6

6 free-range chicken breasts (I prefer to use chicken with the skin on, as you get more flavour, but for a lower fat content, use skinless chicken breasts)

For the marinade:

2 tablespoons natural yoghurt
2 tablespoons cream
1 tablespoon paprika
½ teaspoon garam masala
½ teaspoon chilli powder
½ teaspoon ground cumin
½ teaspoon salt

½ teaspoon turmeric
2 tablespoons lemon juice
2 tablespoons sunflower oil
1 tablespoon tomato purée
2 cloves of garlic, crushed
1 teaspoon fresh ginger, grated
(grates easier if placed in the freezer for 10 minutes)

For the Bombay Potatoes:

1 kg peeled, cubed potatoes
1 tablespoon sunflower oil
2 onions, finely chopped
1 tablespoon tomato purée
2 tablespoons black mustard seeds

1 tablespoon curry powder
Salt and freshly ground white pepper
150 ml vegetable stock
100 g baby spinach

For the Mango Salsa:

1 large mango, peeled and chopped
1 red chilli, deseeded and chopped

Juice of 1 lime
1 tablespoon chopped mint

Combine all the marinade ingredients and marinate the chicken breasts overnight.

To cook, preheat the oven to 200°C/400°F/gas 6. Heat a frying pan with 2 tablespoons of sunflower oil. Seal the chicken breasts and transfer to the preheated oven for 25 minutes. Place the potatoes in a saucepan with cold water, bring to the boil and drain immediately.

Meanwhile, in another saucepan heat the sunflower oil and fry the onions.

Add the tomato purée, mustard seeds, curry powder and salt and pepper. Cook for 1 minute, stirring with a wooden spoon. Add the potatoes and vegetable stock. Cover and cook for 10 minutes, until the potatoes are tender. Add the baby spinach just before serving.

To make the salsa, mix all the ingredients together.

Serve the chicken on top of the Bombay Potatoes, garnished with Mango Salsa and Tzatsiki (p. 34).

Chicken and Chorizo Stew

This dish is an easy, cheap way of serving a lot of people. It can be made in advance and reheated. This stew is excellent with Corn Bread (p. 43).

Serves 6

100 g chorizo sausage, sliced 3 mm thick
2 onions, sliced
12 cloves of garlic with skin on
6 chicken legs with thigh and skin on
100 g plain flour
1 tablespoon sweet paprika
2 tablespoons olive oil

250 ml chicken stock
250 ml white wine
1 sprig of rosemary
2 tablespoons stoned kalamata olives
400 g chickpeas, cooked
1 x 400 g tin chopped tomatoes

Preheat the oven to 190°C/375°F/gas 5. Heat a large casserole dish on the stove. Add the chorizo and brown. Add the onions and garlic. Toss the chicken legs in the flour and paprika. Shake to remove excess flour. Heat a frying pan. Add the olive oil and sauté the chicken legs until golden brown. Remove to the casserole. Add the chicken stock, wine and rosemary. Bring to the boil, cover and place in the oven. Remove after 1 hour and add the olives, chickpeas and chopped tomatoes. Return to the oven for 30 minutes. Remove, check seasoning and serve.

Braised Pork Belly Served with Pea Champ, Caramelised Apple and Calvados Jus

Serves 6

Start this dish the day before you are serving it.

For the meat:
1.3 kg boneless, rindless pork belly
4 onions, sliced
1½ litres chicken stock

For the marinade:
250 ml soy sauce
100 g pickled ginger (available in Asian markets)
1 head of garlic, peeled and broken into cloves

For the Calvados Jus:
175 ml apple juice   *300 ml jus (p. 31)*
1 shot of Calvados   *150 ml cream*
1 small sprig of rosemary   *Salt and freshly ground black pepper*

For the Caramelised Apple:
2 Granny Smith apples   *Salt and freshly ground black pepper*
30 g butter   *¼ teaspoon sugar*

For the Pea Champ:
Allow 1 large peeled potato per person
500 g frozen peas or 1 tin of mushy peas, drained
100 ml milk
100 ml cream
50 g butter

For the marinade, mix the soy sauce and pickled ginger together.

Score the fatty side of the pork belly at 1 cm intervals. Do this diagonally to get a nice criss-cross pattern. Divide the pork into 6 pieces. Place in a container and cover with the marinade. Add the garlic cloves and place in the fridge for at least 24 hours.

To cook, preheat the oven to 200°C/400°F/gas 6. Remove the pork from the marinade and pat dry with kitchen paper. Keep the marinade. Season with pepper – there is enough salt in the soy sauce. Heat a large frying pan and fry the pork until golden brown, then place in an ovenproof dish. Fry the onions in the pan and add to the pork. Bring the marinade and chicken stock to the boil in the frying pan. Pour over the pork. Cover tightly with tinfoil and place in the oven for 2 hours.

To make the Calvados Jus, reduce the apple juice to one-third in a saucepan, until it resembles a syrup. Add the Calvados, rosemary and jus. Bring to the boil, add the cream and check the seasoning before serving. Do not boil at this stage, or the sauce may split. To make the Caramelised Apple, core the apples, leave the skin on and cut each apple into 12 segments. Heat a frying pan, add the butter and toss in the apples. Season with salt and pepper and sprinkle with sugar. Cook until golden brown over a medium heat. If you think the apples may burn, sprinkle with water.

To make the Pea Champ, place the potatoes in cold, salted water and bring to the boil. Turn down the heat and cook until tender. Drain. Keep the potatoes in a saucepan and cover with a clean tea towel to dry. Meanwhile, cook the peas, drain and purée in a blender. Heat the milk, cream and butter in a saucepan. Add to the potatoes and mash until creamy. Add the blended peas and mix well. To serve, slice the pork belly and place on top of the Pea Champ. Cover with Caramelised Apples and spoon the sauce over the meat.

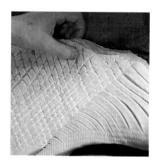  

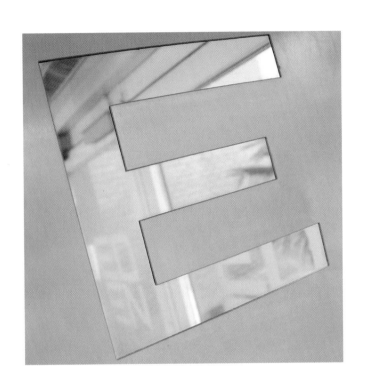

Beef and Guinness Stew

Serves 6 to 8

Marinate the meat for 1 or 2 days before making the stew. The meat needs to have a fat content for flavour and texture, so get advice from your butcher. We use meat from the shoulder, and source organic beef from O'Toole's of Terenure.

1 kg diced stewing beef
225 g onion, diced
225 g carrot, diced
225 g celery, diced
300 ml Guinness
1 litre jus (p. 31)

1 sprig of rosemary
1 sprig of thyme
225 g button mushrooms
(if large, cut into quarters)
60 g butter
Mashed Potato (p. 168), to serve

For the marinade:
4 cloves of garlic, sliced
1 teaspoon paprika
1 sprig of thyme

1 sprig of rosemary
200 ml Guinness – we use the canned
Guinness draught

Mix all the dry marinade ingredients together. Rub into the beef, then add the Guinness. Cover, place in the fridge and marinate the beef overnight. To cook, preheat the oven to 200°C/400°F/gas 6. Drain the beef from the marinade and pat dry with kitchen paper. (We will not reuse the liquid from the marinade, as it will cloud the stew.) Heat a large frying pan and brown off the meat in small amounts; you want to seal it on all sides to hold the texture. Remove from the pan and put in an ovenproof dish. Fry the onion, carrot and celery in the pan. Add the Guinness and jus. Bring to the boil and pour over the meat in the ovenproof dish. Add the rosemary and thyme and cover tightly with tinfoil. Place in the oven and cook for 90 minutes, until the beef is tender. Before serving, heat the butter in a frying pan and cook the mushrooms until they are brown and tender. Add to the stew and serve in bowls with Mashed Potato (p. 168).

So You Don't Eat Meat

Asparagus, Pea and Feta Quiche

Makes 4 individual or one large quiche

For the pastry:

350 g flour

135 g butter

Pinch of salt

2 egg yolks

1 tablespoon white vinegar

50 ml cold water

For the filling:

1 bundle of asparagus, trimmed and blanched

100 g diced feta

200 g frozen peas, cooked

½ tablespoon chopped mint leaves

4 eggs

200 ml cream

100 ml milk

10 g butter (to grease tins)

To make the pastry, combine the flour, butter and pinch of salt in a bowl. Add the egg yolks, vinegar and water. Bring together into a ball using your hands. Do this as quickly as possible, as overworked pastry becomes tough. Wrap in cling film and place in the fridge to rest. To make the pastry tartlets, preheat the oven to 200°C/400°F/gas 6. Roll out the pastry on a lightly floured surface. Grease a 30 cm fluted quiche tin or 4 individual tins with butter. Line the tins with the pastry and prick the base with a fork. Place in the freezer for 15 minutes. This will help stop the pastry from shrinking. Remove from the freezer and line with parchment paper. Fill with any dried beans to weigh it down. Place in the oven and bake for 10 minutes. Remove the beans and paper and return to the oven for 5 to 7 minutes, until golden brown. Remove from the oven and leave in the tin. Cut the asparagus spears into 3 or 4 pieces. Mix with the feta, peas and mint. Divide between the tartlets. Mix the eggs, cream and milk in a jug and season. Pour the egg mix into the tart. Bake in the oven until the filling is puffed up and golden brown. This will take about 30 minutes for a large tart and 15 minutes for individual tarts.

Alternative fillings:

Chopped tomato and kalamata olives

Roast peppers and goat's cheese

Fennel Salad

Serves 4

We make a number of variations of this salad. The following are just three of them. Serve on their own or as a base for a chicken or blue cheese salad. Delicious!

2 bulbs of fennel, very finely sliced
Juice of 1 lemon
4 tablespoons olive oil
Salt and freshly ground white pepper

The fennel must be very finely sliced. You can use a mandolin for this, which can be purchased in an Asian market or kitchen shop. Always use the guard or you will have shaved finger salad. Combine all the ingredients in a bowl and allow the flavours to develop for 20 minutes before serving.

Variations:
Add 100 g sliced button mushrooms.
Add 50 g rocket leaves, 1 sliced pear and 50 g crumbled blue cheese.
Add 2 blood oranges, segmented, and 50 g chopped roasted hazelnuts.

Welsh Rarebit

Serves 4

One of my favourite snacks, brunch dishes or appetisers in winter.

250 g Cheshire cheese
200 ml beer
1 large teaspoon English mustard
Ground white pepper
4 thick slices of bread
Butter

Slice the cheese thinly into a saucepan. Cover with the beer and add the mustard and pepper. Place over a low heat and stir constantly until smooth and runny. Preheat the grill. Toast 4 slices of bread and butter them. Place each slice of toast on a heatproof plate. Coat each slice with the cheese mixture and brown under the grill for 3 to 4 minutes. Serve hot.

Ratatouille

Serves 4

Great hot or cold as a vegetable dish. We also use this as a base for lasagne or as a filling for Filo Parcels (p. 208) with a tin of drained chickpeas added.

2 tablespoons olive oil
1 red onion, peeled and finely diced
2 cloves of garlic, crushed
1 aubergine, diced about 1 cm in size
2 courgettes, diced about 1 cm in size
1 red pepper, deseeded and diced
1 yellow pepper, deseeded and diced
Salt and freshly ground black pepper
500 ml Tomato Sauce, approx. (p. 32)
2 tablespoons chopped basil

Heat the oil in a heavy-based saucepan. Add the onion and garlic and cook for 3 minutes. Add the remaining vegetables and season with salt and pepper. Cook on a low heat for 5 minutes. Add the Tomato Sauce to cover and cook for a further 5 minutes. Add the basil and serve. If you wish, you can roast all the vegetables individually tossed in olive oil before you add them to the pan. This is more time consuming but will give a better texture.

Baked Flat Mushrooms with Herb and Shallot Breadcrumbs

Serves 6

Allow 1 large or 2 small flat mushrooms per person
Olive oil to drizzle over mushrooms for cooking
Salt and freshly ground black pepper
90 g butter
3 shallots, finely chopped
3 cloves of garlic, crushed
300 g fresh white breadcrumbs
3 tablespoons chopped fresh herbs – we use a mixture of sage, parsley, thyme and tarragon

To serve:
100 g rocket leaves
Balsamic vinegar
Extra virgin olive oil
60 g Parmesan cheese, shaved

Preheat the oven to 180°C/350°F/gas 4. Place the mushrooms on a roasting tray, brown side up. Drizzle with olive oil and season. Place in the oven for 12 minutes, until cooked. Remove from the oven but leave on the tray. Meanwhile, melt the butter in a saucepan and add the shallots and garlic. Cook over a low heat until soft, but not brown. Mix the breadcrumbs and herbs in a bowl. Add the butter from the a saucepan and mix through. Divide the stuffing between the mushrooms, return to the oven and heat through. This will take about 10 minutes. To serve, toss the rocket leaves in balsamic vinegar and extra virgin olive oil. Divide onto serving plates. Place the mushrooms on top of the leaves and garnish with Parmesan shavings. (To shave Parmesan, use a sharp knife and pull it along the block of Parmesan or use a vegetable peeler to get thin slices.)

Braised Fennel with Orange and Cardamom

Serves 4

1 tablespoon sunflower oil
3 bulbs of fennel, cut into quarters
150 ml white wine
Zest of 1 orange
2 cardamom pods
1 star anise
1 tablespoon chopped ginger
Juice of 2 oranges
Salt and freshly ground white pepper

Heat a saucepan. Heat the oil, then add the fennel and cook for 5 minutes, until golden brown on all sides. Add the remaining ingredients and bring to the boil. Reduce the heat and cover. Cook over a low heat for 30 minutes, until tender.

Celeriac Lasagne with Gruyère Cheese

Serves 4

2 whole celeriac, peeled and cut into slices about 3 mm thick
Olive oil   200 g baby spinach
½ tablespoon butter   1 quantity of Ratatouille (p. 147)

1 quantity of Ratatouille (p. 147)

For the cheese sauce:
Olive oil   2 tablespoons white wine
1 clove of garlic, crushed   200 ml cream
2 shallots, finely chopped   100 g grated Gruyère cheese

Preheat the oven to 200°C/400°F/gas 6. Brush the celeriac slices with olive oil and place on a baking sheet. Do not overlap. Place in the oven for 15 to 20 minutes. To make the sauce, heat a little olive oil in a saucepan. Add the garlic and shallots and cook until soft but not brown. Add the white wine and reduce by half over a medium heat. Add the cream and again reduce by half over a medium heat. Add the grated cheese. Do not allow to boil at this stage or the sauce will split. To assemble, butter an ovenproof dish (30 cm x 30 cm). Lay a layer of roast celeriac slices on the bottom. Cover with some baby spinach, then add a layer of Ratatouille. Repeat the process 3 or 4 times, depending on the depth of the tray. Finish with a layer of celeriac and cover with the cheese sauce. Place in the oven and cook for 40 minutes. You can also use individual tian rings to make individual servings. These will look more formal and take a shorter time to cook, approximately 15 minutes.

Couscous

Serves 4 to 6

500 g couscous
4 tablespoons olive oil
Juice of 4 lemons
Salt and freshly ground pepper
500 ml vegetable stock
3 tablespoons chopped mint
3 tablespoons chopped parsley

Rinse the couscous in cold water. Add the olive oil, lemon juice and seasoning and stir well. Add the boiling stock and stir. Cover with cling film and allow to stand for 10 to 15 minutes, until tender. Remove the cling film and mix well with a fork. To finish, add the chopped mint and parsley. To make a more substantial dish, you can add finely diced red onion, peppers and cress.

Tabbouleh

Serves 4

This is made using cracked bulghur wheat.

110 g bulghur wheat
Vegetable stock to cover wheat (approx. 200 ml)
125 ml extra virgin olive oil
Juice of 1 lemon
Salt and freshly ground white pepper

Rinse the bulghur wheat well in cold water. Place in a bowl. Pour in boiling stock to cover the wheat. Cover the bowl with cling film and leave to stand for 25 minutes, until wheat is tender. Remove the cling film and drain off any excess liquid. Add the olive oil, lemon juice and salt and pepper. The tabbouleh is now ready to serve.

You can also add the following to improve texture and flavour:
2 tablespoons chopped mint
2 tablespoons chopped parsley
2 tablespoons finely diced red onion
4 tablespoons chopped scallions
1 red pepper, finely diced

Cashel Blue Polenta

Serves 4 to 6

Olive oil
1 onion, peeled and finely diced
2 cloves of garlic, chopped
1.2 litres vegetable stock
300 g coarse polenta
60 g Cashel Blue cheese, crumbled
30 g butter
1 teaspoon salt
1 sprig of thyme
Fennel, Pear and Walnut Salad (p. 118), to serve
Peperonata (p. 24), to serve

Grease a flat baking tray. Line with parchment paper and brush with olive oil. Preheat the oven to 200°C/400°F/gas 6. Heat a saucepan and add the olive oil. Cook the onion and garlic until soft, but not brown. Add the stock and bring to the boil. Using a whisk, swirl the water and pour the polenta into the centre. Stir well with a wooden spoon and cook over a low heat for 12 minutes, until it is thick and gloopy. Add the cheese, butter, seasoning and thyme leaves. Pour the polenta onto the baking sheet. Place in the oven for 10 minutes. Allow to cool by placing in the fridge to set for 2 to 3 hours and cut into triangles.

To serve, heat a frying pan with the butter. Gently fry the slices of polenta on both sides. Serve on a warm plate with Fennel, Pear and Walnut Salad (p. 118) or Peperonata (p. 24).

Spanish Tortilla

Serves 6

This is one of my favourite brunch dishes. We serve it with pepper relish and a plate of cheese, charcuterie and roast vegetables. It's an easy brunch, as it can be made in advance. You will need a deep (6 cm), large (28 cm diameter) frying pan to make this. The frying pan must be ovenproof.

2 tablespoons olive oil
3 large Rooster potatoes, peeled and diced into 1 cm cubes
1 white onion, finely sliced
2 cloves of garlic, peeled and sliced
100 ml cream
7 eggs

Heat a deep-fat fryer to 130°C/265°F. Fry the diced potato until cooked but not coloured. Remove, drain on greaseproof paper and cool. Heat a frying pan and add the olive oil. Add the onion and garlic and cook until soft but not brown. In a bowl, mix the cream and eggs together. Add the potatoes to the egg mixture and season. Pour into the pan over the onions. Cook over a low heat until the first side is cooked, about 7 to 10 minutes. The tortilla should be quite solid at this stage. Use a plate to turn the tortilla by sliding the tortilla onto the plate and then returning to the pan upside down. If this process scares you, do not attempt it, just finish the tortilla in the oven without turning. This will take 5 to 10 minutes. Allow to cool for 10 to 15 minutes before you attempt to cut it.

Roast Root Vegetables

Serves 6

We normally roast celeriac, carrots, celery and parsnips with whole garlic cloves. Each vegetable cooks at a different speed, so it's better to place them in the oven at different times.

Preheat the oven to 200°C/400°F/gas 6.

For roasting, use the following amounts for each vegetable:

1 sprig rosemary
1 sprig thyme
1 tablespoon honey or maple syrup (optional)
1 or 2 tablespoons olive oil
1 tablespoon butter
Salt and freshly ground pepper

For parsnips, celery, carrots and celeriac use 450 g of each vegetable. Peel and cut the vegetables into 4 cm sticks. Remove the woody centre of the parsnips if necessary. Toss each individual vegetable in the honey, oil, butter and herbs. Season with salt and pepper. Place in individual ovenproof dishes.

Carrots take 35 minutes to cook.
Celeriac takes 30 minutes to cook.
Celery takes 20 minutes to cook.
Parsnips take 20 minutes to cook.

Toss regularly during roasting to stop the honey from sticking. For the roasted garlic, place 20 cloves of unpeeled garlic in a saucepan of boiling water and cook for 15 seconds. Drain and cool with cold water. Continue to cook as with the other vegetables. Garlic takes 15 minutes to cook.

Before serving, you can mix all the vegetables together.

Risotto

Serves 4

This is another Eden staple, on its own as an appetiser, supper dish or served with scallops or fish. We use Arborio rice, a starchy rice that absorbs a lot of liquid and gives you a lovely, creamy result while retaining a bit of bite.

Time and patience along with the correct ingredients are all you need to make a perfect risotto every time. A heavy-based casserole or a saucepan is also essential. Have the stock at a slow boil all the time – it makes it easier for the rice to absorb the liquid.

Basic recipe:
1.3 litres vegetable stock
2 tablespoons olive oil
2 shallots, peeled and finely diced
300 g Arborio rice
100 ml white wine
50 g butter
50 g grated Parmesan
Salt and freshly ground white pepper

Put the stock in a saucepan and bring to the boil. In a heavy-based saucepan/casserole, heat the olive oil. Add the shallots and cook until soft, but not brown. Add the rice and stir well with a wooden spoon so that the rice is well coated with the oil. Add the wine and stir until the wine is absorbed. Using a 200 ml ladle, add the stock, one ladle at a time to the rice. After each addition of stock, stir continuously until the liquid is absorbed before you add another ladle of stock.

Please don't be tempted to add the liquid too quickly – good food takes time.

Once you have added three-quarters of the stock, check the rice to see if it's al dente, i.e. not chalky but still with a little bite. If still hard, continue to add the stock. To finish, turn off the heat. Add the butter and Parmesan, stir and cover. Allow to stand for 10 minutes. Risotto can be garnished with Parmesan Crackling (p. 170).

Risotto Variations:

Tomato, Chorizo and Basil

Cook 100 g diced chorizo in a pan. Remove the meat, then cook the shallot in the chorizo oil. Continue as per basic recipe. Before serving, add the chorizo, chopped tomato and shredded basil to the risotto after it has rested for 10 minutes.

Pea and Mint Risotto (see Scallops, p. 91)

Lemon and Garden Herbs

Before serving, add the juice and zest of 1 lemon and 3 tablespoons of freshly chopped mixed herbs, such as chives, chervil and parsley.

Roast Peppers and Goat's Cheese

Roast 2 red peppers and peel and dice. Before serving, add the peppers and 60 g crumbled goat's cheese to the risotto.

Thyme, Rocket and Pecorino Cheese

Add 100 g grated Pecorino cheese instead of Parmesan. Also add 1 dessert-spoon of picked thyme leaves and 100 g rocket leaves.

Quesadilla

Serves 4

I made these first with Johnny Cooke and still love how easy and versatile they are. A great party dish. These can be made in advance and stored in the fridge before cooking.

Allow 2 soft flour tortillas per person

For the filling:
500 g brie, sliced
1 pineapple, peeled, cored and thinly sliced
2 red chillies, deseeded and sliced
60 g sliced jalapeño peppers, to garnish
60 g crème fraîche, to garnish

Place 4 tortillas on the work top. Divide the filling ingredients between the 4 tortillas. Cover with the remaining tortillas. Heat a large frying pan. Add a little oil and butter, just enough to glaze the pan. Carefully place the assembled quesadilla in the pan and brown on each side. Cook until the cheese begins to melt. Remove from the pan and cut into quarters. Serve with jalapeño peppers and crème fraîche.

Alternative fillings:
Pear, blue cheese and walnut
Mango, brie and chilli
Cooked spiced chicken strips with grated cheddar

Mashed Potato

Serves 6

1 kg peeled Rooster potatoes
150 ml milk
150 ml cream
60 g butter
Salt and white pepper
Grated nutmeg (optional)

Place the peeled potatoes in a saucepan (the potatoes should be as evenly sized as possible). Cover with cold water and add a little salt. Bring to the boil and gently simmer until cooked. If you cook them too quickly, the potatoes will break up. Drain and cover with a clean tea towel to dry out. Heat the milk, cream, butter and seasoning in a pan. Do not boil. Mash the potatoes and add the liquid. Mix with a wooden spoon until smooth. Check seasoning and serve.

Variations:
Add 100 g chopped spring onions
2 tablespoons wholegrain mustard
1 tin of drained mushy peas
200 g shredded cabbage, cooked in butter
200 g chopped leeks, cooked in butter
Roasted and mashed head of celeriac added to mash

Lentils du Puy

Serves 4

Great on their own or as a base for Confit of Duck Leg (p. 131), sausages, breast of chicken, lamb, cod or salmon.

2 tablespoons olive oil
1 tablespoon butter
1 onion, peeled and finely diced
2 cloves of garlic, crushed
1 carrot, peeled and finely diced
2 celery stalks, finely diced
1 leek, white part only, finely diced
200 g lentils du puy, soaked in water overnight
1 sprig of thyme, picked
250 ml approx. vegetable stock
Salt and freshly ground pepper
100 g baby spinach leaves

Heat the oil and butter in a heavy-based saucepan. Add the diced onion, garlic, carrot, celery and leek. Fry until golden brown. Add the lentils and thyme, coating with the oil. Add enough stock to cover. Cook for 7 to 10 minutes. Season with salt and pepper. Drain the liquid, add the baby spinach and serve.

Grilled Asparagus with Mushroom Duxelle, Hollandaise Sauce and Parmesan Crackling

Allow 5 spears of asparagus per person

For the crackling:
180 g grated Parmesan
90 g grated cheddar

For the mushroom duxelle:
80 g butter
80 g shallots, peeled and finely chopped
400 g button mushrooms, wiped and finely chopped
350 g flat mushrooms, wiped and finely chopped
Salt and freshly ground pepper

1 x Hollandaise Sauce (p. 5)

Use young green asparagus, otherwise break off the end of the stem if it's old and woody. Bring a large saucepan of water to boil. Add the salt and asparagus. Bring back to the boil and cook for 2 to 3 minutes. Remove the asparagus and place in iced water to stop it cooking; you want the asparagus to be green and crunchy. To make the duxelle, heat a heavy-based saucepan and add the butter. Once foaming, add the shallots. Cook until soft, but do not brown. Add the mushrooms and cook on a gentle heat until soft and liquid has evaporated. Season. For a smooth paste, this mixture can be liquidised.

For the crackling, preheat the oven to 200°C/400°F/gas 6. Mix both cheeses together. Spread the cheese evenly in a 10 cm circle on a non-stick silicone baking mat. Do 4 at a time. Place in the oven and bake for 5 to 7 minutes, until golden brown and crisp. Remove with a palate knife and place over a rolling pin while still warm to give a nice curved shape. To serve, reheat the asparagus under the grill. Place 5 spears on each plate. Put 2 spoons of mushroom duxelle at the base of the asparagus spears, drizzle with hollandaise sauce and garnish with Parmesan Crackling.

Gratin Potato Dauphinoise

Serves 6

This can be served immediately from the oven or made the day before and cooled with a weight on top. You can then cut it into triangles or circles with a tian ring if you wish.

50 g butter
1 kg Rooster potatoes
Salt and freshly ground pepper
500 ml cream
2 cloves of garlic, crushed
Freshly grated nutmeg
175 g grated cheddar

Preheat the oven to 200°C/400°F/gas 6. Grease an ovenproof dish with butter. Peel the potatoes and slice into thin circles. (We use a mandolin for this.) Place the potatoes in the greased ovenproof dish and season with salt and pepper. Heat the cream in a saucepan with the garlic and nutmeg. Pour over the potatoes and cover with tinfoil. Place in the oven and bake for 40 minutes. Remove the foil and sprinkle with the cheese. Return to the oven for another 10 minutes, until the cheese is golden brown.

Celeriac Bake

As an alternative we make this with a mix of 500 g potato and 500 g celeriac or 1 kg of celeriac. Use 250 ml cream and 250 ml coconut milk. Omit the cheese and the nutmeg and add a finely chopped red chilli instead. It is an unusual, tasty twist on this traditional dish.

Gnocchi

Serves 4

1 kg potatoes (we use Roosters; this will yield 750 g cooked potato)
75 g soft butter
120 g strong flour
4 egg yolks
Salt and freshly ground white pepper
50 g semolina

Preheat the oven to 200°C/400°F/gas 6. Bake the potatoes in their skins until cooked. Remove from the oven, peel and mash. Cool slightly. Add the butter, flour and egg yolks to the warm mashed potato. Season. Place a saucepan over a low heat. Add the potato mix and cook until smooth and shiny. When ready, the mix will come away from the sides of the pot. Cool slightly. Place the mix in a piping bag with a 1 cm plain nozzle. Sprinkle work surface with semolina. Pipe long strips of mix onto the work surface. Cut into 2 cm lengths. Unusually, we pan-fry the gnocchi in butter; this gives a golden, crisp outside and a soft centre. It can also be cooked in boiling salted water until the pieces float to the top.

To serve, toss the gnocchi in:
A simple tomato sauce with basil and grated Parmesan cheese.
Melted butter with chopped sage and grated Parmesan cheese.
Heat 200 ml cream in a saucepan; reduce the volume by half and add 100 g grated blue cheese. When melted, add the gnocchi.

Filo Parcel with Moroccan Spiced Vegetables

Serves 4

8 sheets filo pastry
45 g melted butter

For the filling:
4 tablespoons olive oil
6 cloves of garlic, crushed
1 red chilli, deseeded and finely chopped
1 tablespoon chopped fresh ginger
2 teaspoons coriander seeds, ground
2 teaspoons cumin seeds, ground
¼ teaspoon ground cinnamon
2 teaspoons mustard seeds
200 g onion, peeled and finely diced
200 g carrots, peeled and finely diced
200 g butternut squash, peeled, deseeded and finely diced
200 g celery, finely diced
100 g cooked French beans, chopped into 3
Grated rind of 1 orange
90 g toasted almond flakes
Salt and freshly ground white pepper

Preheat the oven to 200°C/400°F/gas 6. Heat a saucepan with the sunflower oil. Add the onion, garlic, chilli, ginger and spices. Cook for 4 minutes. Place all the other vegetables and grated orange rind in a roasting tin. Pour the mix from the saucepan over the vegetables and mix well. Cover with tinfoil and place in the oven for 30 minutes. Remove and allow to cool. Add the flaked almonds and green beans. Turn the oven temperature down to 180°C/350°F/gas 4.

To assemble, melt the butter. Lay 4 sheets of filo pastry on a work top. Brush with butter. Lay another sheet on top of each sheet. Cut in half widthways. Divide the mixture in 4 and place in the centre of the pastry.

Brush the edges with melted butter and bring the edges together in a bundle to resemble an alms purse. Bake on a greased tray for 25 minutes.

We serve these with Couscous (p. 154) and Red Pepper Relish (p. 27).

Alternative fillings:

Mushroom Duxelle (p. 170) with sliced, cooked asparagus and toasted cashew nuts

Ratatouille (p. 147) with chickpeas

Pumpkin and Peanut Curry with Pilaf Rice

Serves 4

For the curry:
4 tablespoons sunflower oil
800 g pumpkin or butternut squash, peeled and diced
1 onion, finely diced
2 celery stalks, finely diced
1 carrot, peeled and finely diced
Salt and freshly ground white pepper
4 cloves of garlic, crushed
1 tablespoon chopped fresh ginger
2 red chillies, deseeded and finely diced
2 tablespoons crunchy peanut butter
1 teaspoon tomato purée
1 x 400 ml can coconut milk
Zest and juice of 1 lime
1 tablespoon soy sauce
1 tablespoon fish sauce (optional)
1 x 400 g tin butterbeans, drained
1 tablespoon chopped coriander leaves, to garnish

For the rice:
1 tablespoon sunflower oil
2 tablespoons finely diced onion
200 g basmati rice
Salt and freshly ground pepper
1 litre vegetable or chicken stock
1 tablespoon chopped parsley, to garnish
1 tablespoon chopped roasted peanuts, to garnish

Preheat the oven to 200°C/400°F/gas 6. Heat a roasting tin with 2 tablespoons of sunflower oil. Add the diced pumpkin, toss well and place in the oven. Roast until tender but not mushy, about 20 minutes.

Meanwhile, heat the remaining oil in a large a saucepan. Add the onion, celery and carrot and cook for 15 minutes until soft but not brown. Season with salt and pepper. Add the garlic, ginger, chilli, peanut butter and tomato purée. Stir well and cook for a further 5 minutes. Stir occasionally to prevent it from sticking. Add the coconut milk, lime zest and juice, soy sauce and fish sauce. Bring to the boil and check the seasoning. Add the pumpkin and butterbeans. Reheat for 5 minutes.

To make the rice, heat an ovenproof dish on the stove. Add the sunflower oil. Add the onion and cook for 3 minutes, until soft. Add the rice and coat well with the oil. Season with salt and pepper, add the stock and bring to the boil. Cover and place in the oven for 12 minutes. Check to see if the rice is soft and all the liquid has been absorbed.

To serve, divide the rice between 4 warm plates. Place a ladle of curry on top of each. Garnish with chopped coriander and peanuts.

Ice Cream and Puddings

Ice Cream Base

Serves 8

170 ml milk
200 ml cream
1 vanilla pod, split lengthways and scraped
6 egg yolks
270 g caster sugar

Gently heat the milk, cream and vanilla pod in a saucepan. Mix the egg yolks and sugar in a large bowl with a balloon whisk. When the cream/milk mixture comes to the boil, pour over the egg mix and whisk. Rinse the saucepan with cold water and strain the mixture back into the saucepan. Return to a low heat and cook slowly, stirring constantly, until the mix coats the back of the spoon. Be careful, as the mixture can scramble at this time. Remove from the heat and pour into a bowl. Cool quickly; we place the bowl with the ice cream base in a dish of iced water. This is the basic ice cream recipe. Before churning in an ice cream machine, we add 175 ml cold cream and 175 ml stock syrup to make Eden vanilla ice cream.

For the stock syrup:
250 ml water
175 g caster sugar

Place both ingredients in a saucepan. Melt the sugar over a low heat, then bring to the boil. Allow to reduce slightly and cool. Store in the fridge.

Chocolate Ice Cream

Serves 10

200 g dark chocolate, at least 60% cocoa
75 ml cold cream
1 x basic ice cream recipe (p. 182)
125 ml stock syrup (p. 182)

Break the chocolate into a bowl. Bring the cream to the boil and pour over the chocolate; stir constantly until fully melted. Add the ice cream mix and then the stock syrup and churn in an ice cream machine. For added richness, add a shot of chocolate liqueur before churning.

Passion Fruit and Mango Ice Cream

Serves 10

6 passion fruits
1 mango
1 x basic ice cream recipe (p. 182)
175 ml cold cream
125 ml stock syrup (p. 182)

Halve the passion fruits and scrape out the seeds and juice. Strain using a sieve and keep the juice. Discard the seeds, as when frozen, they can break teeth! Peel the mango and remove the stone. Purée the mango and passion fruit juice in a blender. Add to the ice cream base mix with the cream and stock syrup. Churn in an ice cream machine. To serve, peel and slice a mango thinly. Splash with vodka and sliced chilli and serve with ice cream – unusual but delicious.

Strawberry Ice Cream

Serves 10

300 g washed and hulled strawberries
100 g caster sugar
1 x basic ice cream recipe (p. 182)
125 ml stock syrup (p. 182)
175 ml cold pouring cream

Cut the strawberries in half and place in a saucepan. Sprinkle with the sugar and allow the strawberries to gently soften over a low heat. Remove from the heat and cool fully. In a large bowl, mix the ice cream base with the stock syrup and the cold cream. Mix well. Churn this mix in an ice cream machine until half-frozen; this will take about 20 minutes. Remove from the ice cream machine and add the cold strawberries and syrup from the saucepan. Pour into a container and further set in the freezer. This will give you a lovely texture of strawberries through the ice cream.

Maple Ice Cream

Serves 10

1 x basic ice cream recipe (p. 182)
175 ml pouring cream
125 ml maple syrup

Mix all ingredients together. Transfer to an ice cream machine and churn for 20 minutes. Transfer to a container and put in the freezer to set completely.

Banana Nut Brownies

Serves 6

175 g butter, cut into cubes
300 g light muscovado sugar
175 g dark chocolate (70% cocoa solids)
100 g chopped walnuts
3 eggs, beaten
2 ripe bananas, mashed
100 g self-raising flour
2 tablespoons cocoa powder
1 teaspoon baking powder

Preheat the oven to 200°C/400°F/gas 6. Butter and line a 20 cm square tin with silicone paper. Place the butter, sugar and chocolate in a heatproof bowl over a pot of simmering water. Stir until melted and remove from the heat. Cool slightly. Stir in the nuts, eggs and bananas until well mixed, then sift in the flour, cocoa and baking powder. Mix gently.

Pour into the prepared tin and bake for 50 minutes, until firm to touch in the centre. Remove from the oven and cool in the tin. To serve, cut in squares and serve with cream, Chocolate Sauce (p. 188) or ice cream.

Brownie mix can also be crumbled and added to the basic ice cream mix (p. 182) at the end of churning to make brownie ice cream.

Chocolate Sauce

Serves 6

250 g chocolate, minimum 60% cocoa solids
60 g caster sugar
350 ml water
50 ml pouring cream

Grate the chocolate into a saucepan. Add the sugar and water and bring to the boil. Reduce the heat and simmer for 15 minutes. Remove from the heat and add the cream. Whisk well and serve.

Irish Strawberries with Lemon Yoghurt Sorbet

Serves 6

A wonderful summer dessert, light and refreshing.

1 kg strawberries, washed, hulled and cut into quarters

For the sorbet:

100 g sugar	*150 ml cream*
100 ml water	*50 g honey*
400 g full-fat organic natural yoghurt	*juice and rind of 1 lemon*

To make the sorbet, place the sugar and water in a saucepan. Dissolve the sugar over a low heat, bring to the boil and then allow to cool completely. Mix all the remaining ingredients together and churn in an ice cream machine. Store in the freezer. To serve, place the strawberries in a large martini glass. Top with a scoop of sorbet and garnish with a sprig of mint.

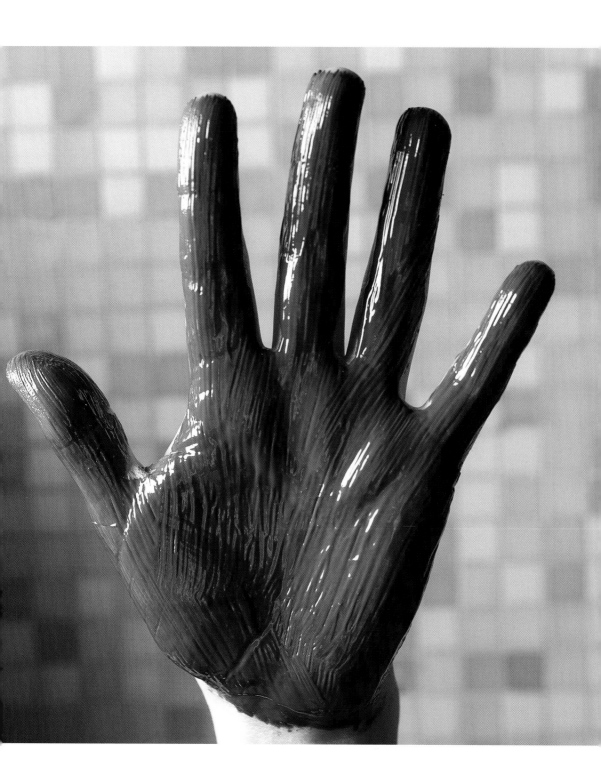

Hazelnut Pannacotta

Serves 8

3 leaves of gelatine
250 ml milk
225 g caster sugar
900 ml cream
50 g hazelnut purée
Toasted hazelnuts, to serve

Soak the gelatine leaves in cold water; they will become soft and spongy.
Place the milk, sugar and cream in a saucepan. Heat gently to dissolve the
sugar and bring to the boil. Add the hazelnut purée and simmer on a low
heat for 15 minutes. Remove from the heat and allow to stand for 5 minutes.
Add the gelatine and stir to dissolve. If you add the gelatine when the
mixture is too hot, it may cook and become lumpy. Strain into a jug and
then pour slowly into ramekins. Chill until set, about 4 hours. Serve with
toasted hazelnuts.

Chocolate, Bailey's and Hazelnut Parfait

Makes 6

We set these in pyramid-shaped rubber moulds. These are available in good kitchen shops and are worth buying if you are interested in food presentation.

150 g melted chocolate, 60% or higher cocoa content
2 eggs and 4 egg yolks
225 g caster sugar
4 leaves of gelatine
360 ml softly whipped cream
100 g chopped, roasted hazelnuts
2 tablespoons Bailey's

For the caramel sauce:
250 g granulated sugar
25 ml + 250 ml water

Using a clean pastry brush, paint the inside of each mould with the melted chocolate. Allow to harden and repeat the process. Using an electric mixer, whisk the eggs and egg yolks at a high speed until light and fluffy.

Meanwhile, place the sugar and 2 tablespoons of cold water in a saucepan over a low heat. Dissolve the sugar and then bring to the boil. When there are large bubbles on top, it is ready to add to the egg mixture. Add very slowly in a trickle with the speed of the mixer on low. Return to a high speed and beat until the egg and sugar mix is cool. Soak the leaves of gelatine in cold water. When soft and spongy, squeeze any excess water out. Add the gelatine to the egg and sugar mixture. Mix thoroughly. Fold the softly whipped cream into the mixture and add the hazelnuts and Bailey's. Spoon the mix into the chocolate-lined moulds and place in the freezer to set, about 3 hours. It can also be set in individual glasses or ramekins. To make the caramel sauce, place the sugar and the 25 ml of water in a heavy-based saucepan. Dissolve the sugar over a low heat and then bring to the boil. Cook until it turns an amber colour. Remove from the heat and carefully add the 250 ml of water; do not splash, as sugar burns are very sore. Return to the heat to allow any lumps to dissolve. Cool totally before using. When cold it will have a consistency like honey and will keep in the fridge for a week. To serve, place a spoon of caramel sauce on the plate. Loosen the chocolate pyramid from the mould using a sharp knife. Place on the plate and garnish with a Sable Biscuit (p. 199). If set in a ramekin or glass, do not remove and serve with a Sable Biscuit on top.

Apple and Cinnamon Crumble

Serves 6

We make ours in three layers using tian rings 4 cm high and 7 cm in diameter. You can also make this in 1 large spring base tin at least 4 cm high and 23 cm in diameter.

For the frangipane:

240 g butter

240 g sugar

60 g plain flour

180 g ground almonds

4 eggs

For the fruit mix:

8 large Granny Smith apples

120 g caster sugar

2 level teaspoons ground cinnamon

For the crumble topping:

150 g plain flour

90 g butter

90 g caster sugar

30 g porridge flakes

30 g nibbed almonds

For the frangipane, cream the butter and sugar in a bowl with a wooden spoon. Mix the flour and almonds together. Add 1 egg with a spoon of the almond/flour mix into the butter and sugar mixture. Mix and continue to add the 4 eggs like this. Once finished, refrigerate. Peel, core and dice the apples, about 1 cm in size. Place the apples, sugar and cinnamon in a saucepan and cook gently for 5 minutes. Strain and cool. For the crumble topping, place the flour in a bowl. Rub the butter into the flour using your fingertips until it looks like breadcrumbs. Add the sugar, porridge flakes and almonds and mix.

To assemble, preheat the oven to 190°C/375°F/gas 5. Place 8 tian rings on a baking tin covered with silicone paper. Line the base of each tian ring with 1 soupspoon of frangipane. Spread out to the edge and a quarter way up the side of the tian ring. Fill the ring three-quarters full with the fruit mix. Cover with the crumble. Place in the oven and bake for 40 minutes. If cooking in a large ring, it will take 65 minutes. Remove from the oven and cool for 15 minutes in the tian ring, then remove from the ring using a sharp knife to loosen the edge. Serve warm, or it can be cooled and reheated. Serve with Toffee Sauce (p. 196) and/or softly whipped cream.

Toffee Sauce

50 ml water
200 g granulated sugar
200 ml pouring cream

Place the water and sugar in a saucepan over low heat. Dissolve the sugar, then bring to the boil until it turns a nut brown colour. Add a quarter of the cream and remove from the heat. Stir to remove any lumps. Add the remaining cream and allow to cool before serving.

Crème Brûlée

Serves 6

Patience is a virtue, and is required for this dish.

6 large egg yolks
140 g caster sugar
500 ml cream
1 vanilla pod, split lengthways and scraped
6 x 8 cm ramekins

Preheat the oven to 120°C/250°F/gas 2. Mix the egg yolks and sugar in a bowl. Place the cream and vanilla pod in a saucepan and heat very, very slowly. Bring it just to boiling point. Pour the cream onto the egg yolks, whisking all the time. Allow to sit until a skin forms on top. Remove the skin with a spoon and discard. Using a ladle, place the mix in ramekins. Place the ramekins in a deep baking tray. Pour hot – not boiling – water into the tray to two-thirds of the way up the ramekin. Place the tray in the oven and cook for 30 minutes. Check if it's cooked by pressing the top gently with your finger; it should still be slightly wobbly. Remove from the oven and tray and allow to cool. Before serving at room temperature, sprinkle a spoon of sugar over the top and caramelise under a hot grill or using a blow torch.

Dark or White Chocolate Mousse

Serves 6

3 leaves of gelatine
540 g white chocolate or 540 g dark chocolate
500 ml softly whipped cream

For the anglaise:
230 ml milk
230 ml cream
Vanilla pod
4 egg yolks
150 g sugar

To make the anglaise, gently heat the milk, cream and vanilla pod in a saucepan. Mix the egg yolks and sugar in a large bowl with a balloon whisk. When the cream/milk mixture comes to the boil, pour over the egg mix and whisk. Rinse the saucepan with cold water and strain the mixture back into the saucepan. Return to a low heat and cook slowly, stirring constantly, until the mix coats the back of the spoon. Remove from the heat and pour into a bowl.

Soften the gelatine leaves in water. Squeeze to remove any excess water and add to the anglaise mix. Stir to dissolve. Place the chocolate in a bowl and melt over a saucepan of boiling water. Make sure the water doesn't get into the chocolate. Pour the anglaise into the chocolate mixture and stir until mixed through and smooth. Fold in the softly whipped cream.

This mousse is very versatile. You can set it in individual glasses, tian rings, one large bowl or in filo pastry baskets (p. 208). We serve the white chocolate mousse with raspberries and Sable Biscuits (p. 199).

Sable Biscuits

Makes 20

400 g unsalted butter
200 g caster sugar
1 egg yolk

500 g plain flour
1 teaspoon vanilla extract

Preheat the oven to 190°C/375°F/gas 5. Beat the butter and sugar together. Add the egg yolk, flour and vanilla and bring together into a ball using your hands. Do not over-mix. Wrap in cling film and place in the fridge for 1 hour. On a lightly floured surface, roll out the pastry until quite thin. Cut into shapes using cookie cutters. Place on a baking sheet covered with silicone paper. Bake for 15 to 20 minutes, until golden. Remove from the oven and allow to cool on the tray. Store in an airtight container.

Lemon Drizzle Cake

Makes 2 loaf cakes

For the cake:
175 g caster sugar
175 g self-raising flour
100 g soft butter
1 teaspoon baking powder

2 eggs
90 ml milk
Zest of 1 lemon

For the drizzle:
100 g caster sugar

Juice of 1 lemon

Preheat the oven to 190°C/375°F/gas 5. Grease and flour 2 x 2-lb loaf tins. Put all the cake ingredients into a bowl. Using an electric mixer, beat until it is pale and fluffy. Pour into both tins and bake for 40 minutes.

To make the drizzle, dissolve the sugar in the lemon juice. Spoon over the cakes as soon as they come out of the oven. This can be served as a cake or used as a dessert with strawberries and ice cream.

Pistachio Tuiles

Makes 10

These are a great accompaniment to the Dark Chocolate Mousse (p. 198). These are also excellent served with ice cream.

150 g unsalted butter
150 g icing sugar
150 g liquid glucose
50 ml milk
200 g chopped pistachio nuts
100 g nibbed almonds

Preheat the oven to 190°C/380°F/gas 5. Heat a saucepan and add the butter, sugar, glucose and milk. Bring to the boil and boil for 2 minutes. Remove from the heat and add the chopped nuts. Put into a bowl. Allow to cool completely. This paste can be made in advance and kept for 3 days in an airtight container in the fridge. Roll a teaspoon of the paste into a ball between your palms. Place well apart on a baking tray lined with parchment paper. Bake until they spread out and are dark brown in colour. If undercooked, they will not harden.

To serve, set the mousse in tian rings. You can serve a tuile flat on the bottom and top of the mousse, making a sandwich. Alternatively, as soon as the tuiles come out of the oven, you can roll them around the handle of a wooden spoon to make a shape like brandy snaps, or finally, cool them over a rolling pin to give a lovely curved shape.

Glossy Chocolate and Peanut Butter Tart

Serves 8

A chocolate and nut delight for those who love desserts; not at all cloying as you might expect with peanut butter.

For the base:
500 g crushed digestive biscuits
30 g nibbed almonds
120 g melted butter
2 tablespoons maple syrup

For the peanut mix:
360 g cream cheese
120 g caster sugar
1 jar crunchy peanut butter
300 ml softly whipped cream

For the chocolate topping:
60 g caster sugar
300 ml cream
240 g chocolate (55% cocoa solids)
30 g butter

Preheat the oven to 180°C/350°F/gas 4. Grease and line a 23 cm spring base tin with silicone paper. Mix all the ingredients for the base together and evenly spread on the base of the tin. Place in the oven for 15 minutes. Remove from the oven and cool fully in the tin. For the peanut mix, cream the cheese, sugar and peanut butter together until smooth. Fold in the cream and pour over the biscuit base. Allow to set.

For the chocolate topping, place the sugar and cream in a saucepan. Place over a low heat, stirring to dissolve the sugar. Bring to the boil, reduce the heat and cook for 3 minutes, until it's a pale yellow colour. Add the chocolate and stir until melted. Add the butter and mix. Cool slightly and pour over the tart. Leave to set in the fridge. Remove from tin. Remove paper and serve.

Blueberry and Coconut Pudding
with Lemon Curd or Berry Compote

Serves 6

120 g butter
120 g caster sugar
90 g plain flour
½ teaspoon baking powder

2 eggs
90 g desiccated coconut
3 tablespoons blueberries

For the lemon curd:

225 g unsalted butter
225 g caster sugar

Zest and juice of 3 lemons
5 egg yolks

For the berry compote:

400 g mixed berries (you can use frozen berries)
100 g caster sugar
1 teaspoon vanilla extract

Preheat the oven to 190°C/375°F/gas 5. Grease a 20 cm ovenproof dish. In a food mixer, beat the butter and sugar together until light and fluffy. Sieve the flour and baking powder onto a plate. Crack the eggs into a bowl and mix together with a fork. Add a little egg and some flour to the butter mix. Continue to do this until all the egg and flour mix has been added. Lastly, fold in the coconut and blueberries. Pour into the greased dish and place in the oven. Bake until golden brown, about 25 minutes. The pudding is cooked if it springs back when touched. To make the lemon curd, put the butter, sugar, lemon juice and zest in a heatproof bowl. Fill a saucepan with water and bring to the boil. Reduce the heat and sit the bowl on top of the saucepan. Once the butter has melted, beat well with a balloon whisk until totally mixed. Add 1 egg yolk at a time and continue to cook over the water until thick. This will take about 20 minutes. Pour into a clean jar and cool. Cover with a tight lid. This will hold in the fridge for 2 weeks. For the berry compote, place the berries, sugar and vanilla in a saucepan over a medium heat. Allow the sugar to dissolve, then cook the berries until soft but still holding their shape. Serve the pudding warm with a spoon of curd or compote on top. Berry compote is also excellent with ice cream.

Eden Mess

Serves 6

A quick and easy dessert, best made the day before serving.

225 ml cream
500 ml thick natural yoghurt
225 g chopped strawberries

4 meringue nests, crumbled
100 g toasted almonds
Splash of cassis (optional)

Whisk the cream and yoghurt together until thick. Add the strawberries and crumbled meringues. Stir in the almonds. Place in 1 bowl or 6 individual ramekins. Place in the freezer overnight. Remove from the freezer to the fridge 1 hour before serving. Serve with Sable Biscuits (p. 199).

Lemon Surprise Pudding

Serves 6

This pudding is excellent served with Berry Compote (p. 204) and softly whipped cream.

150 g caster sugar
75 g butter
Zest of 1 large lemon
3 large eggs, separated

Juice of 2 lemons
40 g plain flour
225 ml milk

Grease an ovenproof dish (1200 ml in size) with butter. Sit in a deep baking tray filled halfway up with hot water. Preheat the oven to 190°C/375°F/gas 5. Using a food mixer, beat the sugar and butter together until light and fluffy. Add the lemon zest and egg yolks and mix. Add the lemon juice. The mix may look curdled at this stage, but don't worry, it won't affect the final product. Using a whisk, gently beat in the flour and milk. In a separate bowl using a clean whisk, beat the egg whites until they stand in white fluffy peaks. Fold the egg whites into the pudding mix. Pour into the buttered dish. Bake until the pudding has risen and springs back to the touch, about 45 minutes.

Almond Chocolate Chip Cake

Serves 6

200 g butter
200 g caster sugar
4 medium eggs
200 g chocolate, at least 60% cocoa
50 g plain flour
1 teaspoon baking powder
1 teaspoon vanilla extract
180 g ground almonds

Preheat the oven to 190°C/375°F/gas 5. Line the base of a 20 cm cake tin with parchment paper and grease with butter. In a food mixer, beat the butter and sugar together until white and creamy. Break the eggs into a small bowl and mix lightly with a fork. Chop the chocolate into fine pieces but not dust. Sieve the flour and baking powder onto a plate. Add a little of the egg and a spoon of the flour to the butter and sugar mix. Continue to do this until all the egg and flour has been added. Add the vanilla extract and ground almonds to the mix. Fold in gently. Finally, add the chocolate and mix gently. If you over-beat the mixture at this stage you will have a heavy, flat cake. Pour into the prepared tin and bake for 40 to 45 minutes. The cake should be firm to the touch and if you insert a metal skewer into the centre it should be clean and not sticky when removed. It may have some melted chocolate on it but should not have cake mix on it. Remove from the oven and leave to cool for 15 minutes in the tin, as the cake may break up if you try to take it out of the tin too soon. This cake can be served warm as a dessert with softly whipped cream.

Filo Pastry Baskets with Toffee Bananas, Maple Pecan Nuts and Ice Cream

Serves 4

Filo baskets will hold in an airtight container for 3 days. They can also be used as an edible bowl in which to serve ice cream, strawberries, mousse or fruit salad.

4 bananas
1 x Toffee Sauce (p. 196)
1 x Maple Ice Cream (p. 185)

For the baskets:
1 packet filo pastry (you will find this in the freezer section of the supermarket)
Icing sugar, to dust
120 g butter, melted

For the maple toasted pecans:
100 g pecan nuts
3 tablespoons maple syrup
You will also need 4 ramekins, a clean, damp tea towel and a pastry brush

Preheat the oven to 180°C/350°F/gas 5. Defrost the pastry and carefully unfold, as the pastry is brittle. Cut through all the sheets together, into 4 quarters. Cover with a damp towel. Dust the work surface with the icing sugar. Turn 4 ramekins upside down and brush with the melted butter. Take 4 sheets of pastry and place on the icing sugar. Brush each one with butter and layer on top of a ramekin. Place each sheet at a different angle so that it resembles a star. Each ramekin should have 4 layers. Place on a baking sheet and cook until golden brown, about 12 minutes. Continue with this process until you have enough filo baskets. Cool on a wire rack and store in an airtight container. To make the maple toasted pecans, line a baking tray with silicone paper. Place the pecans on the paper and roast in the oven for 10 minutes. Remove, toss the nuts in maple syrup, spread out on the paper again and return to the oven for 3 minutes. Remove from the oven and cool. To assemble for 4 people, place a filo basket on each plate. Heat the toffee sauce and slice 4 bananas into the sauce and remove from the heat. Stand for 3 minutes and divide into the baskets. Place a scoop of ice cream in each basket and sprinkle with the pecans.

Praline and Cherry Ice Cream Sandwich with a Caramel Sauce

Serves 8

This is a fantastic dessert for a dinner party, as you can make it in advance and serve directly from the freezer.

200 g black cherries
100 ml kirsch

1 x ice cream base recipe (p. 182)
Caramel Sauce (p. 192), to serve

For the sponge:
5 eggs, separated
25 g + 100 g caster sugar

60 g ground almonds
60 g flour

For the praline:
200 g granulated sugar
50 ml water
50 g roasted whole hazelnuts with skin off
50 g roasted whole almonds with skin off

Remove the stones from the cherries and soak in the kirsch for 30 minutes. To make the sponge, preheat the oven to 190°C/375°F/gas 5. Line 2 baking trays (30 cm x 40 cm approx.) with silicone paper. Whisk the egg whites and 25 g sugar in a large, clean bowl until they are white and peaky.

Place 5 egg yolks and the remaining sugar in a large bowl sitting over a saucepan of boiling water. Whisk using a handheld beater or balloon whisk until double in size and white in colour. Add the sieved almonds and flour to the mix and fold in very gently – **do not beat**. Fold in the egg white mix gently or the sponge will be tough. Spread the mix over the 2 trays and bake for 8 to 10 minutes, until golden brown in colour. Remove from the trays and cool. Remove the paper and cover with a clean tea towel to keep from drying out. To make the praline, line a baking tray with silicone paper. Put the sugar and water in a heavy saucepan. Place on a low heat and dissolve the sugar. Increase the heat and bring to the boil until nut brown in colour. Add the roasted nuts and pour onto the prepared baking tray. Cool completely, then place in a plastic bag and bash with a heavy saucepan to break up into crumbs. This can also be done in a food processor. Store in an airtight container. Place the ice cream base in an ice cream machine and churn for 15 minutes. Add the crushed praline and churn for a further 10 minutes. This can be assembled in individual tian rings. To serve 8 people, cut 16 rings of sponge using the tian ring. Place the rings on a tray that will fit in your freezer. Line each tian with a circle of sponge. Cover with a layer of cherries. Add a layer of ice cream to fill the tian ring almost to the top. Cover with another ring of sponge and press down gently. Cover with cling film and freeze. To serve, remove from the ring using a sharp knife. Serve with caramel sauce and the remaining cherries. We also serve this with roast peaches.

Roast Peaches

Preheat the oven to 190°C/375°F/gas 5. Halve the peaches and remove the stones. Rub the flesh with butter and place on a baking sheet. Drizzle with sweet dessert wine and bake for 12 minutes, until soft but holding their shape.

Sheridan's Cheese

Introduction

Cheese is the most wonderful food; from a single ingredient comes an infinite variety of tastes and textures. It is one of the most nutritious foods, providing almost all the nutrients we need to survive. It is an ancient convenience food ready to be eaten without any preparation. It is the most versatile cooking ingredient, used in sauces, sandwiches, soufflés, bakes and a thousand other dishes. And on its own with a glass of wine, it can be the ultimate gourmet experience.

Choosing Your Cheese

Over the past few years, it has become easier to find good-quality cheese around Ireland. There are more and more independent speciality food shops springing up around the country, many of which provide a decent range of cheese. Food markets have enabled specialist retailers and cheese makers to sell in areas where there might not be enough demand to have a shop all week. And even the supermarkets have improved their range.

When you are shopping for cheese, try to buy it from a retailer who will allow you to taste it first; your eyes will never tell you as much as your taste buds. Preferably buy your cheese freshly cut or as individual small cheeses – cheese does not like to spend several weeks wrapped in plastic in refrigerated storage. Also, the distributors of such pre-packed cheeses tend to choose the cheeses not on their taste quality, but rather their ability to withstand the large distribution network. Generally cheeses with a boring appearance will have a boring flavour. Pure, unblemished white rinds, smooth plastic coatings, straight edges and perfectly symmetrical rounds tend to portray industrially made cheeses with little character, whose main functions are to fit in boxes and look good on shelves.

If you are buying cheese to serve as part of a meal, don't be constrained by common perceptions of what a cheese board should be. The general idea is to serve a selection of cheeses which will offer you and your family or guests contrasting flavours and textures. Ideally, a cheese board should have a nice soft white-rinded cheese, a blue cheese, a hard cheese and a washed rind cheese (they're the smelly ones with the pinkish rinds), and if possible a sheep's or goat's milk cheese. However, it's better to have one gorgeous cheese than five mediocre pieces.

Storing Your Cheese

Cheese is a living, breathing food and needs to be treated with some care to get the best from it, particularly softer cheeses. The ideal scenario is to buy your cheeses from someone who has cared properly for them and then serve them that evening. However, this isn't always practical, so here are a few tips on keeping cheese. The first and most important rule is to always serve cheese at room temperature – serving it cold substantially inhibits the flavour. If you're able to buy the cheese on the day it will be eaten, just leave it out of the fridge until that evening.

Unfortunately, very few of us now have the luxury of a cellar or cold larder where cheese would be at its happiest, so we have to improvise. A good place to store cheese can be an unheated room or garage. But don't worry too much, fridges aren't as bad for cheese as they are sometimes made out to be, and their main fault is their dry atmosphere rather than the cold temperature. Ensure your cheese is well wrapped in a breathable covering such as wax paper. This is particularly important for cheeses with mould or culture rinds and fresh goat's cheeses; plastic will suffocate them and often cause off-flavours.

Serving Your Cheese

Once again, the most important rule here is that the cheeses are served at room temperature. If you're storing them in the fridge, take them out at least an hour before you intend to use them. Aside from this, there are no rules. Some people like to have their cheese before dessert and others prefer it after; it's up to you. With regards to accompaniments, I think it's good to serve something which will act as a foil against the richness of the cheese and clean the palette between cheeses. Fruit is perfect for this. Fresh, ripe fruit is ideal, such as ripe pear or apple. However, avoid unripe fruit. Instead you could serve a chutney, fruit jelly or dried fruit. When it comes to choosing between bread and crackers, I would always prefer nice crusty yeast bread, but better still, don't choose – serve both.

A question that vexes many people is whether they should eat the rind of the cheese or not. Again, there is no rule here as it's a matter of personal taste, but I will give my opinion. For hard cheeses, the rind is generally not good to eat, as it is mostly too hard except for the most determined; it can also taste pretty awful! For cheeses with a more delicate mould or culture rind, this is generally edible. However, edible does not always mean pleasant. If you do like eating the rind, please taste the paste first without the rind, as the flavour of the rind is more intense and can overpower the more delicate nuances of the paste. If you are discarding the rind, try to take off as little as possible, as the flavour of the cheese tends to change from the centre to the surface. The flavour of the cheese just under the rind is often the most interesting.

Wine and Cheese

This is a very popular subject on which many people will willingly give a full thesis. However, I am not such a person. It is indisputable that wine and cheese go very well together and can often bring the best out of each other, enhancing some flavours and softening others. My advice on this subject is simple – enjoy the research! The pleasure here is in the experiment. Never be afraid to try new combinations. There are no rules and many great surprises.

Cheese Types

What makes a cheddar different from a Camembert, an Emmental from a blue cheese? I will try to give an easy and quick explanation of the different cheese types.

Of course, these different types are very general and there are many crossovers and variations. The type of milk used also makes a difference. Any mammal's milk can be used, but the main ones are cow, goat and sheep. Each animal's milk has different qualities which lend themselves to particular cheese-making methods and produce a different cheese when common methods are used. Other variances in cheeses are caused by the climate and terrain where the animals are raised and the time of year the cheese is made. Differences also occur if the cheese-maker pasteurises the milk or leaves the natural cultures in the milk.

Hard cheeses

As the name suggests, these cheeses have a firm texture, such as cheddar, Parmesan, Gruyère and Gouda. These cheeses are matured slowly and can often be aged for several years. Their rind tends to be smooth, with very little mould or culture. The flavour in these cheeses develops slowly with age. The paste gets stronger and drier as the cheese ages. Of course, there are many different varieties depending on the tradition in which it is made.

Traditional English cheeses such as cheddar and Lancashire are made in a particular way, adding salt to the curd and pilling the curds on top of each other before they are wrapped in cheese-cloth to mature, resulting in a slightly crumbly, acidic cheese. European cheeses such as Gruyère, Emmental and Parmesan are called thermophilic cheeses because the curds are heated slightly to give a smooth texture and sweeter flavour.

There are many more varieties, but almost all types of hard cheese originated due to the need to store milk, which was plentiful in summer, and preserve it for winter and for transport to towns and cities. The differences between the cheeses tend to stem from different ways of reducing the moisture content of the curd which helps to preserve it; these methods include cutting the curd into tiny pieces, pressing the curd using weights and heating the curds to expel moisture. The flavour tends to be more subdued than in cheeses with active rinds, but they can develop full, strong flavours, ranging from sweet and nutty to sharp and tangy.

White-rinded cheeses

These are cheeses such as Brie and Camembert. They have a white mould growing on the surface of the cheese. This mould does two things – it softens the paste of the cheese and it develops the flavour. You can see this develop if you look at the paste of one of these cheeses before it is fully ripe. The paste just under the skin will be soft and the centre will be chalky. This is because the cheese has not been matured for long enough. As the cheese ages, the rind affects more and more of the paste until it is soft to the centre.

These cheeses are not made to last and are usually fully ripe in five to eight weeks, depending on the size. You will notice that most of these cheeses are made in flat, thin wheels. This shape allows the mould to ripen the cheese to the centre before it becomes over-ripe under the rind. These cheeses tend to have a mushroomy, vegetable type of flavour and of course a soft, creamy texture.

Washed-rind cheeses

These cheeses have a bacterial or cultural rind, predominately made up of a culture called B-Linens. They are the ones with a pinkish colour and they often smell a little. Examples of this type would be Durrus and Gubbeen from Ireland and the classic French cheeses Pont l'Eveque and Munster. These bacteria love a lot of moisture but are very delicate, so during maturation, the cheeses are washed with water which sometimes contains alcohol or a little salt, which protects it from unwanted moulds. Thus, the name washed-rind.

The culture rind acts in a similar way to the white mould on a Camembert, softening the paste and developing the flavour. However, it is not as powerful, and the cheeses tend not to be as soft as the white-rinded cheeses, although this also depends on how much moisture was left in the cheese. This is one of the most popular cheese-making processes and there are many varieties, shapes and sizes. How long the cheese matures for depends on how much moisture it has and whether the cheese-maker has introduced just a little or a lot of these cultures. These cheeses tend to have pungent, earthy and some-times tangy flavours and the texture can vary from quite firm to very soft.

Blue cheeses

Blue cheeses are cheeses in which the growth of a blue/green mould has been encouraged. Famous examples include Roquefort, Cashel Blue and Stilton. A mould called *penicilliumn roqueforti* or *penicilliumn gluacum* is mixed in with the cheese at the start of the production process or during maturation. In order for this mould to grow inside the cheese, it needs to have oxygen, so the cheeses are usually pierced with metal rods. This introduces air to the inside of the cheese and the mould begins to grow. If you look carefully at the rind of a blue cheese you will see little holes where the cheese has been pierced. This process can be combined with many other cheese-making processes, so you can have soft blue cheeses, semi-hard blues and even blue Bries. The intensity of the flavour depends on how much space within the cheese the mould has to develop and how long it is allowed to mature. The flavours tend to be tangy to sharp as well as sweet and often salty.

Fresh and semi-fresh cheeses

These are cheeses where very little is done to the cheese curds and they are made to be eaten quite quickly. There are many varieties, including cream cheese, where fresh, creamy curds are pressed together and packed immediately. Mozzarella is made when the fresh curd is kneaded like dough into balls and packed in whey. Fresh goat's cheeses can be lightly pressed and sold fresh or allowed to grow a natural rind, which develops the flavour. The flavour of these cheeses tends to be delicate and light, but if good raw milk is used

they can have very pleasant, subtle flavours, which should not be mistaken for blandness.

Seasonality

The importance of seasonality in cheeses has diminished as animal husbandry has developed over the last number of decades. However, it is still an important element in the quality of cheeses available at a particular time of year. I think one of the richest qualities of farmhouse foods is its relationship with the seasons. In a world where the consumer must have anything anytime, it is refreshing to find foods which change over the year and some which we can only find at particular times.

Seasonality occurs in cheeses for two reasons. The first is the lactation cycle of the animal. All mammals, of course, have a lactation cycle related to when they raise their offspring. In other words, mammals do not produce milk all year round. Cows generally produce milk for about ten months of the year and the quantity of milk varies during this period. However, with modern herd management, the farmer will have a fairly even milk supply all year. This is achieved by having more than one calving time in the herd. With sheep and goats it is more difficult to get them to breed out of season, although some larger modern dairies do manage to trick their animals into thinking it is a different time of year by adjusting their exposure to daylight hours. In Ireland, however, all the sheep and goat herds still only produce milk seasonally, generally from early spring to late autumn. This means that cow's milk cheeses can be made all year round, but sheep and goat's milk cheeses are not generally made in the winter months. We can still get these cheeses over the winter when they are harder, more mature cheeses.

The second reason for seasonality is the grazing patterns of the animals. Since the only ingredient of cheese is milk, and in turn the milk comes from the grass and other feed which the animals eat, this feed makes a real difference to the final cheese we eat. In Ireland, we are very fortunate that our climate allows for good grass growth for almost ten months of the year. For the other months, Irish cattle are generally fed on silage. The grass that the animals feed on is not constant; the first growth of early spring produces a slightly different cheese to the lush summer growth and the late autumn grass. Each growth can change the fat content of the milk and with each growth there are many different varieties of grasses and herbage, which all combine to give different nuances to the resulting cheeses. Some cheese-makers choose to only use milk from fresh grass for their cheese. These are generally producers of hard cheese who find the milk from silage does not have the same quality. In the mountain regions of Europe, there is still a strong tradition of summer cheese-making. This is where the farmers and often their families move with their animals into high pastures when the winter snows melt. Usually several families combine the milk from their herds to produce large cheeses such as the real Swiss Emmental. These large cheeses are then transported down the mountains and matured, ready to sell during the winter months. There is one very famous cheese, Vacherin Mont d'Or, which is only made in the winter months when the cattle are being fed hay. This relatively small, soft cheese suits the families who have returned from the mountains for the winter. They do not have as much milk available and the soft cheese is easier to transport in the cold winter months.

There are no hard and fast rules about which cheeses are better when. We might think that an Irish soft cheese made in December would be of lesser quality than one from spring milk; for some cheeses they are, but others manage to make really good winter cheese. In general, fresher, softer cheeses tend not to be as good in winter. However, winter can always be brightened by all the goodness and flavour of matured summer milk cheeses. The important thing is to enjoy the different flavours and cheese which the changing seasons bring us.

Whether you are eating cheese in a salad, in a sandwich or as part of an eight-course meal, always look for quality cheeses made by producers whose primary concern is the flavour, not shelf life, packaging or surface appearance. There is no shortage of such cheeses, and thankfully, over the last thirty years, Ireland now produces some of the best.

Fig and Almond Compote

250 g diced dried figs
1 Granny Smith apple, peeled, cored and diced
90 g brown sugar
2 tablespoons brandy
90 g whole almonds
4 tablespoons apple juice

Place the figs, diced apple and sugar in a saucepan. Place on a medium heat and cook for 10 minutes. Add the brandy and cook for a further 5 minutes, until the alcohol evaporates. Remove from the heat. Add the almonds and apple juice and allow to cool. This will keep in an airtight container in the fridge for 1 week.

Cashel Blue and Walnut Crunchies

90 g chopped walnuts
150 g grated Cashel Blue
240 g flour

120 g butter
2 egg yolks

Preheat the oven to 190°C/380°F/gas 5. In a small bowl, mix the walnuts and blue cheese together. In a food processor, mix the flour, butter and two-thirds of the cheese and nut mix together. Hold back the remaining one-third to sprinkle on the biscuits. Add the egg yolks to form a firm paste. Remove and roll in cling film and place in the fridge for 30 minutes. Lightly flour your work surface. Using a rolling pin, roll out the dough to 3 mm thickness. Using a cookie cutter, cut into round shapes. Place on a baking tray lined with parchment paper. Sprinkle the remaining cheese and nut mix on top and bake for 15 to 20 minutes, until golden brown. Allow to cool and store in an airtight container. They will keep for 5 days.

Cocktails

Shot = 35.5 ml measure   **Double =** 71 ml

Caipirinha/Caipiroska

Glass: Tumbler

Garnish: Lime wedge and crushed ice

Ingredients: *4 lime wedges*
                    ¾ shot x sugar syrup
                    ¼ shot x lime juice
                    Crushed ice
                    2 shots x cachaça (Brazilian rum)/Stoli vodka

Method: Put lime wedges into bottom of glass and muddle with
                    spoon to loosen flesh slightly. Add the sugar syrup and lime
                    juice. Fill the glass to the top with crushed ice. Pour the
                    cachaça/vodka over the ice. Stir. Taste and adjust if necessary.
                    Serve with a short straw.

Cosmopolitan/Metropolitan

Glass: Large martini glass

Garnish: Flamed orange zest

Ingredients: *2 shots x Absolut Citron/Absolut Kurant*
                    2 shots x cranberry juice
                    ¾ shot x Cointreau
                    ¼ shot x lime juice

Method: Chill the glass with ice. Half-fill cocktail shaker with ice.
                    Add ingredients according to measures above. Shake
                    vigorously. Empty ice from glass and strain mix into the
                    chilled glass. Garnish.

Martini

Glass: Small martini

Garnish: Customer's choice – olive or twist

Ingredients: *¼ shot x vermouth (the less vermouth, the drier the martini)*
                  2 shots x Stoli Vodka/Bombay Gin

Method: Fill the glass with ice and water and leave to chill. Fill the
                  shaker with ice and, depending on the customer's preference,
                  add a dash or a drop of vermouth to the ice. Stir contents.
                  Strain the vermouth from the shaker so that the ice is coated.
                  Add a double measure of vodka or gin. Working quickly,
                  throw the ice out of the glass and immediately strain the
                  shaker contents into the glass. Garnish and serve as per
                  customer request.

Variations: Dirty Martini – with a teaspoon of oil from the olives
                  Rocks Martini – with ice in a whiskey glass

Dark Chocolate and Orange Martini

Glass: Large martini glass

Garnish: Orange twist

Ingredients: *1½ shots x Stoli vodka*
                  ½ shot x Crème de Cocoa
                  2 shots x orange juice purée/orange juice
                  ½ shot x sugar syrup

Method: Fill the glass with ice and water to chill the glass. Half-fill the
                  shaker with ice and ingredients. Shake vigorously. Empty the
                  ice from the glass. Strain contents into the glass. Garnish
                  and serve.

Espresso Martini

Glass: Large martini glass

Garnish: 2 coffee beans

Ingredients: *2 shots x Absolut Vanilla*
                  1 shot x Kahlúa
                  1 shot x espresso
                  ¼ shot x sugar syrup

Method: Chill glass. Half-fill the shaker with ice. Add all the ingredients
                  to the shaker. Shake very well to get a frothy top. Strain
                  ingredients into the glass, garnish and serve.

French Martini

Glass: Large martini glass

Garnish: Raspberry or blackberry

Ingredients: *2 shots x Stoli vodka*
½ shot x Chambord
2½ shots x pineapple juice

Method: Chill the glass. Half-fill the shaker with ice. Add all the ingredients to the shaker. Shake very well to get a frothy top. Strain ingredients into the glass, garnish and serve.

Apple Strudel Martini

Glass: Large martini glass

Garnish: Apple slice

Ingredients: *1 shot x Absolut Vanilla*
½ shot x cinnamon schnapps
½ shot x sour apple schnapps
½ shot x apple juice

Method: Chill the glass. Half-fill the shaker with ice. Add all the ingredients to the shaker. Shake well. Strain ingredients into the glass, garnish and serve.

Bee's Knees Martini

Glass: Martini

Garnish: Orange wedge

Ingredients: *4 teaspoons runny honey*
               2 shots x gin/Havana Club
               1 shot x lemon juice
               1 shot x orange juice

Method: In the base of the shaker, stir the honey with the gin/Havana Club until honey dissolves. Add the lemon and orange juice, shake with ice and strain into a chilled glass.

Bellini

Glass: Small martini glass

Garnish: Strawberry or red currants

Ingredients: *¼ shot x peach schnapps*
               2 shots x Prosecco
               Splash Crème de Cassis

Method: Chill the glass. Add the peach schnapps. Fill to the top with Prosecco. Dribble Crème de Cassis down the side of the glass so that it sinks to the bottom. Garnish and serve.

Bloody Mary

Glass: Highball

Garnish: Celery stick, lemon, salt rim

Ingredients: *2 shots x Stoli vodka*
                5 shots x tomato juice
                ½ shot x lemon juice
                Tabasco – 4 shakes = rare
                *   6 shakes = medium*
                *   8 shakes = well done*
                Worcestershire – 4 counts
                Salt – 2 pinches
                Pepper – 2 pinches

Method: Half-fill the highball with ice. Add vodka, tomato juice and
                lemon juice. Top with Tabasco, Worcestershire, salt and
                pepper as per customer request. Garnish and serve.

Mojito

Glass: Highball

Garnish: Sprig of mint/straws

Ingredients: *12 mint leaves*
                2 shots x Mount Gay golden rum
                1 shot x lime juice
                ¼ shot x sugar syrup
                Top with soda water

Method: Muddle mint in base of glass using a spoon. Add the rum,
                lime juice and sugar syrup. Half-fill the glass with crushed
                ice and stir. Top up with soda water. Fill top of glass with
                crushed ice.

Margarita

Glass: Martini

Garnish: Salt half rim and lime wedge

Ingredients: *2 shots x tequila*
1 shot x Cointreau
1 shot x lime juice
Dash of sugar syrup, if too sour

Method: Pour all the ingredients into an ice-filled cocktail shaker and shake vigorously to get froth at top. Pour into a chilled glass.

Eden

Glass: Highball

Garnish: Orange peel string

Ingredients: *2 shots x Absolut Mandarin*
½ shot x elderflower cordial
1½ shots x apple juice
Top up with tonic water

Method: Shake the first three ingredients with ice and strain into an ice-filled glass. Top up with tonic water.

Champagne Cocktail

Glass: Flute

Garnish: Orange peel twist

Ingredients: *1 cube of brown sugar*
                3 dashes of Angostura bitters
                ½ shot x Remy Martin cognac
                Top up with champagne

Method: Rub sugar cube with orange peel, then place in base of
                glass and soak with Angostura bitters. Cover the soaked
                cube with cognac and top up with champagne.

Dorian Gray

Glass: Martini

Garnish: Orange zest twist

Ingredients: *1¾ shots x Havana Club rum*
                ¾ shot x Grand Marnier
                1¼ shots x orange juice
                1 shot x cranberry juice

Method: Shake all the ingredients with ice and fine strain into a
                chilled glass.

Elderflower Collins

Glass: Highball

Garnish: Physalis on rim

Ingredients: *2 shots x gin*
                ½ shot x elderflower cordial
                1 shot x lemon juice
                ⅛ shot x sugar syrup
                Top up with soda water

Method: Shake the first four ingredients with ice and strain into an
                ice-filled glass. Top up with soda water.

Pimm's Classic

Glass: Highball

Garnish: Slice of orange, lemon, cucumber, strawberry and sprig
                of mint

Ingredients: *3 shots x Pimm's No. 1*
                Top up with ½ ginger ale and 7-Up

Method: Pour ingredients into an ice-filled glass, stir and serve with
                a straw.

Honeysuckle Daiquiri

Glass: Martini

Garnish: Mint leaf

Ingredients: *4 spoons honey*
                2 shots x Havana Club rum
                1 shot x lemon juice
                1 shot x orange juice

Method: Stir the honey with the rum in the base of the shaker until
                the honey dissolves. Add the lemon and orange juice, shake
                with ice and fine strain into a chilled glass.

Index